The Switch
Life in the Time of Corona

Maha Abboud, MD

With foreword by
Bonniejean Alford

This edition published by Maha Abboud, MD.

Cover design and book layout by Amber Lamarre, Alford Enterprises.
Editing provided by Bonniejean Alford, Alford Enterprises.

All photographs used with permission. Photo credits to Maha Abboud, Bonniejean Alford, Amber Lamarre, Dr. Ammar Bayrakdar, various connections to Maha Abboud, and royalty free purchases from various sites. Illustration on page 66 by Amber Lamarre.

doctormaha.net

ISBN 978-1-7360586-0-2.

I dedicate this book…

*…to the various strong women in my life,
including the one that birthed me and the one I birthed.
They are an endless source of power throughout my life.*

*…to my father and siblings
who have been my lifeboat in an ocean of uncertainty.*

*…to my husband
for his continuous support.*

*…to my home country of Syria,
the land that has given me the pride and spirit to write this book
and give back in hopes of inspiring strength to my fellow immigrants.*

*…to all victims of injustice and COVID-19,
your departure is not forgotten.*

TABLE OF CONTENTS

Foreword

by Bonniejean Alford

When Maha first came to me about writing a book about COVID-19, my first instinct was to run, and it had nothing to do with her expedient timeline. As someone who studies mass trauma events and their impact on society, I simply did not want to look at anything else about this mass trauma event that we were finding ourselves square in the middle of. And it has nothing to do with my personal beliefs about how we responded that were rooted in that twenty years of experience.

My first instinct was present because of that reality that we were, and still are at the time of this writing, square in the middle of something we didn't understand, something we don't understand. Also, there is the knowledge that there is so much more to come that we just don't know yet, which has been the case for many months already. I basically have been forced to become a hermit in the world I love and miss so much. I didn't know if I could handle helping her create something about the very thing that was bringing me personal trauma in the midst of the societal trauma.

It was a huge task Maha asked of me – of herself. She wanted to write this book and share her story from her vantage point as a doctor. She wanted me to assist her in completing the project and bringing it to you, the reader, in a two- to three-month time span, with both of us knowing full well that even if we succeeded at this, the world could change, making everything we had done outdated. To both our sadness, this of course has not happened – this situation continues to live on just as the virus does.

The reality of this book is that what she puts in this writing is rooted in truths that will survive in time. While I still have certain thoughts about the response to this, Maha's book reminded me about how important it is to keep our eyes wide open in any situation. As a doctor, her perspectives give new insight into the importance of good leadership, of community, of being grounded in the land one calls home – even if you have more than one home.

Understanding what being an American is has never been more important than it is right now. It's not about being born here, it's not about being an immigrant, it's not even about living here. Being American is recognizing that even as we expect the world to stay the same, we know that it changes and we must go with that flow. That is how America became what it has become, the flow of that progress has guided us to choices at a societal level by our leaders, choices that have created yet another divide to shape this country.

When Maha came to me, that first instant to run was overshadowed by the curiosity to hear her out. I am so glad I listened to her. I am so glad I took the opportunity to explore something with her from a different perspective than my own or even the conflicting presentations in the media. I am so glad to be a part of the creation of this beautiful interpretation of the world while in the midst of a mass trauma event. Yes, this whole situation has a horrible impact, which is yet to be fully realized.

That is why this book is so important.

It is up to us as citizens, as humans, as Americans, to ensure that the long-term effects of this virus aren't as devastating as they can be. Facts and figures about the mortality rate and infection rate become just numbers and fail to truly measure the magnitude of impact. Each life that is lost, each life that is touched by severe illness, and each life that is touched by the economic, emotional, and physical distancing is a life that matters beyond all else.

I am thankful to have been part of this book, to bring it into your hands because no matter your thoughts about how this all came about, this book offers reality with a touch of beautiful and glorious hope. I would say "enjoy the read," but it's not exactly that kind of a read. I will say this – please have an open mind, take it all in, and listen.

Thank you for reading.

Acknowledgments

A warm wave of gratitude passes through my heart when I think of all the wonderful people I am surrounded by in my life.

First, to my patients, for trusting me enough to share their life stories with me as they allow me to take care of them.

To the smart creative person who is my daughter Sabrina, your choice and use of words never stops surprising me.

To my brothers and my brother-in-law, Dr. Ghassan Abboud, Dr. Amer Abboud, and Dr. Maan Barhoum, your contribution to this book, and on my life in general, is much appreciated.

To my role models and strong support system, my sisters, Dr. Mahasen Abboud, Dr. Nazek Abboud, Dr. Elham Abboud, and Dr. Rinati Abboud, you always keep pushing me forward, especially when I stop, or I look back.

To Amber, who had the magic touch to create a picture out of words.

Last, but certainly not least, to my editor and friend, Bonniejean: without her the book would have never seen the light of day; her free spirit and creativity was an amazing help to shaping my thoughts into words.

Now, I put my book in your hands as the reader, with gratitude and hope that you will get one or two ideas from it to better your life. Because we all can do better.

The Switch

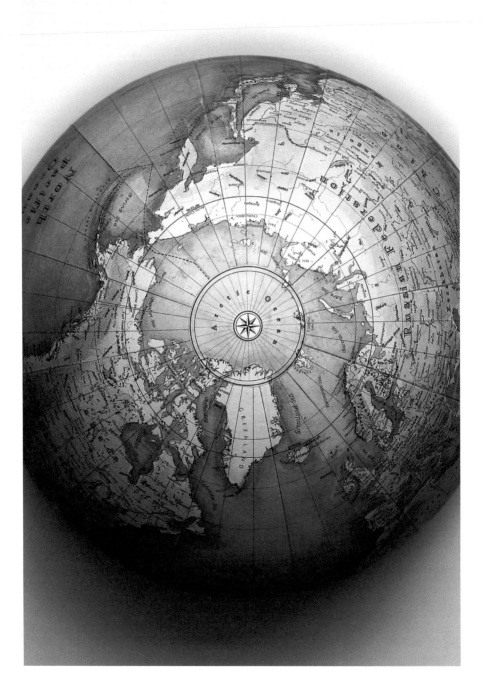

A global switch in life and living - all because of one little virus.

Introduction

Throughout all of history, there has never come a time where the entire globe found itself knowingly affected by the same catastrophe at the same time. Thanks to technology, and all that comes with it, we have a global knowledge where previously we had remained in the dark until long after an event gripped more than one part of the world. In times gone by, usually small countries were more affected by poverty and civil war, while large countries would get into economic quarrels or one of the world wars (I, II, Vietnam, Korea, etc.). These events affected many countries, but not all. Those things that impacted all (i.e. bubonic plague), were seemingly blips in a localized world.

As long as we have kept records, there hasn't been something like this current situation with COVID-19, where we knew it affected the entire world while we were in the middle of the impact. Geographically, every single part of the world has been affected by this. If not by the virus itself, then by the economic hardships that have come as a result of it and the actions taken because of it.

One day during all of this experience, my husband talked to me about how we were witnessing history. With his background of being a social studies and a history teacher, it was fascinating to him, this witnessing of history.

To me it was not fun to watch history again. I've been through enough history. I've been through the Syrian war, which is still ongoing in some parts of Syria. I've been through sirens going off. We were sent home from school to stay in the hallway of our old house, in the city of Homs in Syria. That war between the Arab and Israeli state greatly impacted that corner of my world.

I have witnessed enough history, and I was okay with that. I am okay with that. I didn't need or want to witness more history.

My husband just kept saying, "This is history. We can tell our grandchildren that we witnessed this history. We will tell them stories about this."

I then realized anyone who lived to be seventy years, on average, had witnessed some form of history. World War I, World War II, Korean War, Vietnam Conflict, and many civil wars in different parts of the

Clean up after destruction from the Syrian war - history I lived through.

world. Two neighboring countries attacking each other. We thought we are done with wars, we are smarter than fighting and wars, the UN will help keep peace in the world. And yet, here we are, witnessing history yet again, even if not a war by traditionally-thought standards.

This was a moment in time marking before and after a key world-wide event.

From my vantage point, I have noticed that in the history of humans, few things seem to happen that noticeably impact the world globally, especially within the moment of it happening. Of course, events do have an impact, they just are not addressed as such until years later, if at all.

When I think of global events, I only think of one that is truly recognized on a global scale by Christians and non-Christians alike. That is how we came to say BC and AD, before Christ and after Death of Christ (though sometimes now noted as BCE and CE – Before Common Era and Common Era). This parallel with the BC and AD is what led me to write this book, as told by a simple doctor who came to America seeking the dream life. Originally, I was going to make this parallel with before and after the coronavirus, but ultimately felt that a focus on the switch within everyday practices was a more proper expression of America, and the world's story from within a pandemic.

Now, specifically in America, this luxurious dream of the American life has been turned upside down, switched, if you will, and I am right in the middle of it, witnessing history, yet again.

Life was busy and fast paced before the switch.

The American Life

---◆---

American life is one of the most luxurious in the world. We had it good all along, not knowing how fortunate we were until we started losing it in March of 2020. So many choices, so many options, and yet we always wanted more and more and more.

Choices.

Where do we go for vacation? Should we go to Mexico? Or should we go to Punta Cana? Maybe we should try Costa Rica? Or Brazil? How about Europe? Which country in Europe will be best to visit right now? Which one do we still have on the bucket list that we haven't been to?

When it comes to food, a new restaurant just opened, adding one more to the twenty restaurants already on one street. Seriously, in LaGrange Illinois, where I once lived, on LaGrange Road, there are literally at least twenty restaurants. And now a new one just opened. Let's go try it to please our taste, especially with a new version of food.

A fancy bar just opened too. Not only will the owner give you all kinds of drinks, he will hold classes to teach you how to mix your drink when you are bored at home. As if we need more alcohol to enjoy this life.

How about our kids' activities? We can't have enough, it seems. How many activities should we sign up our kids for? Two. Or three. Or four? More? Which league should we try? Should we do hockey? Or basketball? Maybe tennis or golf? How about baseball? Bowling? Wait, there's two hours on the schedule with nothing going on… maybe we can add chess, or another kind of creative activity to fill up our life.

Those are the choices we took for granted before life changed forever.

When it comes to healthcare, we have so many choices. Your insurance will send you a few hundred doctors you can choose from. If you don't like what this doctor is telling you, you can always go for a second opinion, or third opinion, or more. You can pick up your prescriptions from any number of local pharmacies or, better yet, go to a mail order one.

We cannot forget the houses. Oh, we've been living in this house for 10 years. That's enough. Let's try a new house. Let's try a new neighborhood. Let's try a new state. The options and the choices, unlimited. We can go on and on and on about that American life. Add to it, the television options, a few thousand shows you can choose from. And channels galore: Hulu, Netflix, HBO, HBO Max, Primetime, Amazon. The list could go on. Unlimited access to almost everything you can think of. You think about any crazy show, you will find it. However, the show part of the story of American life became quite handy when we all found ourselves locked at home for a while.

Education.

We cannot forget about the educational choices. Parents have always faced issues like what school to send their kids to. This one, that one? Public school, private school? Should we get them a private teacher? How much playtime are we going to have every week? How many activities? And now, due to the virus, they're faced with an entirely new set of problems since there's no school in the traditional sense.

During these times in 2020, there has been no activity where you can have more than two or three kids together that are not family. This impacted all ages and grades.

For the young, it became a new kind of business as usual, remote learning while parents worked in the next room – had the luxury to work in the next room (at least for some). For college life, the shifts greatly impacted this rite of passage for so many young Americans. Most college students look forward to college, not only for the education they gain, but for all the social aspects of it. College students are busy drinking and hanging out... on the weekends and the weekdays. They're getting to know each other. It's the only part of any American life where people from all over the world get together in one place with little to no judgement – other than to have fun when not studying.

When they go to college, students are no longer only interacting with people who are from their own neighborhood with similar backgrounds because they all live in the same area and they're going to the same school. It's not that anymore. It's college! It's a place

Students studying together before the switch, when students shifted to virtual learning across the country.

where you never know where the student next door in the dorm is from. Or where the one who's sitting in the seat next to you in class is from.

During college, my daughter lived with a student from China and made friends with students from all over the world. This is the promise of college. Students do that. They make friends from everywhere. They get to learn something from each other, they get to interact with each other, bring something to each other's personal growth. Besides learning and trying to find their major, social life is an important ingredient for college. In many ways, the social side is the most important part, as it gives balance to the knowledge.

Of course, many people always think about the economic burden of college. Yes, it is expensive. Many people spend a lot of money for college. To me, even if you don't think the education part of it is worth that investment, it's literally that part of life that no one should miss out on. Experiencing it is worth the investment. You will never have anywhere else for the rest of your life that you can just freely explore, mostly on your terms. You turn 22, you're done with college and life will not be the same. Ever.

College life is so important. Many people have their college friends for the rest of their lives. This aspect of American life has also been disrupted by the virus, possibly more than some other aspects. Students all over America, and the world, actually, are not going to have these experiences this year. Hopefully, only this year.

Before college, parents wait until their young kids go to school. Even in my own practice, many of my patients will say as soon as my kids go to school, I will have my own routine, I will be able to take care of myself. I will go to work. And when they are in their activity or when they are in school, I will get back to my schedule. Summer is hectic, of course, but as soon as the fall comes again and school starts, life returns to a routine. The routine makes life more manageable with regard to all aspects – food, exercise, social life, etc. We can't have this routine right now, not with so much uncertainty in the world, in America.

We cannot forget about the teachers. K-12 teachers enjoy their summer, and it's well worth every minute of it. They work hard during the year. Their school time is not only in school. I lived with a teacher. My father was a teacher. I have seen how much preparation a good teacher needs to do. It takes a lot of their time to prepare for classes. It's almost like working two full time jobs during the school year. They so enjoy their summers off, but many of them are anxious to go back to teach each fall – the weight of the job is heavy.

Over the summers, even as they enjoy their time off, they miss their students. They miss that touch they have on their young lives. They miss the admiration look in their students' eyes when they teach them something they don't know. They miss having the ability to make a difference in their lives.

And right now, many of them are in dilemma since there is so much more to the anxiety than just the workload. They don't know what to do with school. Administrators don't know what to do. Politicians don't know what to do. Everything is unknown. Many teachers are scared. They're scared for their lives and for their students' lives. The anxiety and the fear and the uncertainty are overwhelming, it's going to take over a lot of learning experience – for teachers and students alike.

The classroom will not be the same.

The activities will not be the same.

Just wearing the mask in class will take some of their humanity away. Of course, I'm not saying I'm against the mask, just recognizing the whole point that life is changed completely.

Isn't it sad that we have to cover this beautiful smile?

Beyond the Classroom.

Here in America, so many of us took for granted all we have here. We are grateful for what America has offered us. I know I am grateful for the life I have, and how the busyness of life has driven us, driven me. We often fail to stop and just sit, to think about how lucky we are. At least until the new reality hit us. Now, for better or worse, we have a whole new way of living for the unforeseeable present and future. Obviously, our precious life was not as untouchable as we thought. It was fragile, so fragile. The many flaws in our own lives now also shine through, thanks to the order to stay home in March of 2020, which has given us the chance to reflect on so much about our own life in America.

For me, I have had my share of this good American dream life. America offered me a lot of chances and I have lived the American dream to the fullest. I was fortunate to come across a great opportunity when I finished my medical school from the oldest medical school in the world, Damascus University. Following my studies, I was honored to experience my residency at Mercy Hospital, one of the best hospitals for training in Syria.

Luck or fate stuck me near the end of my residency. My dad was invited to a surprise party for a sister he never met in America. His visit changed him and made me think to expand my education and experience in this magic country, as my father described it.

I came to America, where I entered into a second residency, and a fellowship, in internal medicine and endocrinology. Later, I expanded my specialty into obesity medicine. I was able to build my practice, teach residents, and enjoy my patients, my successes, and my students.

I am forever grateful to the opportunity to come to America and live the dream life. We really had it good. Not only that, for anyone who studies hard and works hard, America is the place for them to succeed. I paved the way for my family to come here, especially the ones who are in the medical and dental fields. They have all made a great life here, with much success, like me and more.

Thank you, America for giving us the opportunity. I hope it comes back, and that as a society, my fellow Americans and I stop taking it for granted – for that is one key lesson that COVID-19 has taught us.

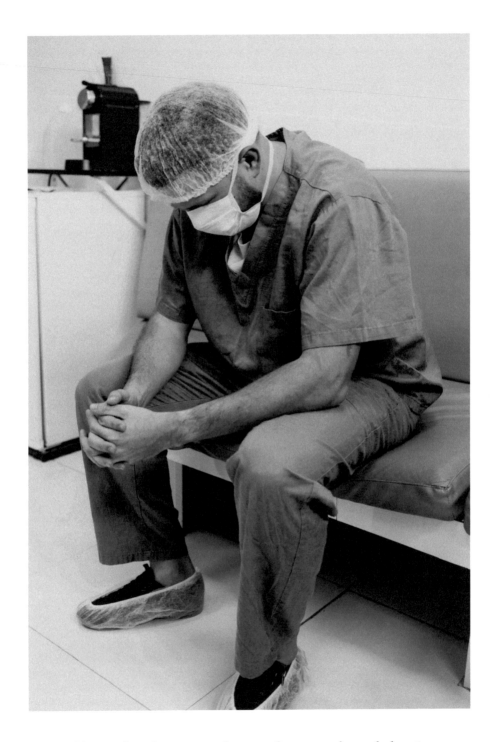

Uncertainty looms as a doctor takes a much needed rest.

The Confusion

Throughout the COVID-19 pandemic, my husband, who as I noted previously was a History teacher in one of his past careers, was having mixed emotions. One of them was concern, because his daughter is a nurse and his wife a doctor. We kept experiencing and seeing and hearing horror stories about how it affected the healthcare workers.

The other part, he was enjoying being part of history.

What bothered me the most in all of this was that many of my patients were dying and I was not taking this COVID-19 situation well. Meanwhile, my husband would say, "Come on, we are part of history. One day we will tell our grandchildren about this. We will tell them we witnessed this."

I repeated to my husband yet again, "I don't want to witness any more history; I've seen enough history."

Enough History.

Being from Syria, I have been through the history of the Syrian war for ten years, and it's still ongoing in some parts of Syria. It was all quite sad. I've been through the history of sirens going off, when we were sent home from school to stay in the hallway of our old house, in the Old City of Homs in Syria, where there was a war between the Arab and Israeli State. I was a small child then, and it was fun because we were released from school and could spend time with family, with cousins. It was fun until the airplanes came, until the attacks started. We waited, witnessing history until it ended. Until we thought it ended.

I don't want to remember those times, yet I do – and so many other parts of history. It is interesting how with specific events you will always remember where you were and how you heard about it. That doesn't change the fact that I have had enough of history.

The history will always stick in your mind, reminding you where you were when you heard some of the major events in your life, or in public life. For example, I remember vividly a time I was doing research and an experiment when I was a fellow at Northwestern. I was having a great time, because what we worked on with this experiment for months had given us wonderful fruit of our hard work. The results of this major experiment, which we might be able to publish somewhere in addition to greatly helping patients, was the highlight of a fellow in the midst of training for a medical life.

I was in the lab, waiting on the last molecular biology reading. It was then that the news came regarding OJ Simpson being acquitted; the verdict came that he was found "not guilty" by the jury. This took all the joy away from me. I felt I was betrayed by America. I used to call America the three Fs: the free, the fair, and the fabulous. I left my own country, my friends, my large loving family, my relatives, my beautiful memory of everything. I left all that for a better life and better education here in America because it's the free, the fair, and the fabulous. When I realized that money would set a criminal free, I was so disappointed. I believed him guilty – many in America did. This outcome of this trial let me down, let many down. I lost faith in the fairness of America, or lack of fairness rooted in money.

Lady liberty has and will always welcome future Americans.

Another historical event in America that I will never forget, none of us ever will: September 11. I remember going downstairs, as I was getting ready to go to work. My husband was up already watching the news with my little one who was one year old at that time. He calmly pleaded, "Please, Sweetie, don't go to work."

"Don't go to the office. Why?"

He said, "Come and see what's happening."

I replied, "I can't not go to work."

Of course, the conclusion came fast that it was a terrorist attack. Somehow, Arabs were the main players in the whole thing. I had to go. I told my husband, "No, I can't miss work. I am the one in charge of my practice. If I'm going to show fear and I'm not going to go to work, what's going to happen to the rest of the staff? What's going to happen to the nervous patients who I need to calm down, even if I am as frustrated, as nervous as they are? I have to go."

My husband had a different thought at that time. He worried greatly for me. You see, when we married, I kept my last name, Abboud. I also used to love airplanes. At the time I was a flight school student. I loved the freedom flying a small plane used to give me when I was little younger. I, of course, didn't think about this, but my husband did. His worry came from the combination of my last name, Abboud, and the reality that I was taking private flying lessons. He was concerned this was not going to play well that day, or over the next several days.

I just laughed. I didn't know what he was talking about. Anyway, the CIA, the FBI, they know everything about me – what did I have to fear? What would I have to fear? So, sure enough, I put on my bravery shoes and went to work.

Yes, I regretted it.

I had no other choice except to go into work. I had three new patients and seventeen return patients. I knew the return patients would not be an issue. In all honesty, I didn't think the new patients would be an issue.

As to my look, before I open my mouth and speak, I can pass for Italian, Greek, or even Hispanic, but at that time, everyone was on high alert.

When I walked in the room, each of these new patients asked me right away, "Where are you from?"

I'm not going to deny my ethnicity, my heritage, so to each I replied simply, "I'm Arabic. I'm from Syria."

Two of the three walked away. The one that stayed became my patient and is still my patient.

I remember those key events in America, as well as others. They stick in my memory, just like I know the memory of these COVID-19 days will stick in my memory long after it is finally resolved and I can go back to living my life, my beautiful "normal" American life, just like everyone else.

The Beginning.

I had a meeting in San Diego during the first week of March. Of course, like anyone who's going to California, I had to take advantage of the trip on a personal side. So, I did, with my daughter and a family friend. We took a few days of vacation before the meeting was to begin. They were to return home as soon as the meeting commenced while I went to the meeting.

We were having fun together, sightseeing, and enjoying the experience. Then, in the midst of our fun, the news broke that the meeting had been cancelled. That every meeting was being cancelled.

More news came that the Los Angeles Airport was closing. The first thing that came to mind was that whoever was in California needed to try to fly home from a different airport as soon as possible – before those airports closed down too. I rushed to book an earlier flight, trying to make sure that I'd be able to get home, worried there would be a cancellation of my new flight. I realized that panic mode was at its highest everywhere, especially administration, travel, hospitals. Responsible people everywhere were in a state of panic – even me.

I could see the panic as I looked at people's faces, the rushing to the airports. Some people began wearing masks. People were running away from each other, no one wanting to get too close to others from the fear of the proclaimed hidden enemy of this new virus.

Thankfully, the three tickets I secured for me, my daughter, and the family friend were not cancelled. We came home early. We hadn't been there long, but had to cut our time short to be home when things got worse – we expected worse.

At the time, the panic mode wasn't as high here in Illinois. I went back to work. The staff was nervous. Patients were nervous. Every visit started taking a little bit longer than it should because patients were asking a lot of questions about the coronavirus (also known as COVID-19). We shared with them what we knew at that point. Although, as you are probably aware, a lot of this knowledge changed fast and constantly.

In March of 2020, the practice was still going, the number of patients declining. The anxiety could be smelled in the air until two to three weeks into March. We began getting all this news about positive, positive, positive, and it hit home. Many of my coworkers were sickened by COVID-19 and they had a hard time getting tested and getting informed with the results when they were tested. At that time, it took fourteen to twenty days for some of them to get the results, whether positive or negative.

We didn't know what was happening.

We were confused.

Then, the official lockdown came.

Always a Doctor.

We had to close the practice physically due to the affected healthcare workers and the lockdown, but the work of a doctor

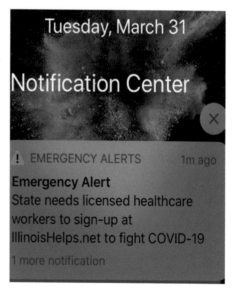

Across the state of Illinois, doctors and non-doctors alike received this notification to register to serve if they were a licensed healthcare worker.

never ends. Some of the staff continued to go in to help us continue to answer questions, send prescriptions, discuss lab results with staff and patients by phone or video visits. When you're a doctor, you're always a doctor. There is no day off.

Meanwhile, the shortage of healthcare workers began to grow – fast.

On March 31, we got the call from the Illinois Governor's Office: all licensed physicians had to report to one place because there would be a shift in need. Some places would need more help. A few of the hospitals was on staff for requested for us to serve as a backup. During those first few weeks, I was not able to be a backup to any hospitals because I needed to take care of my practice while many of our staff were affected. I was the only doctor who didn't get sick.

Thankfully, after those first few weeks, many of my team recovered from having COVID-19 with no serious consequences or sequence. We were then able to support local hospitals. At first, with patient triage and later on with telemedicine and seeing patients for consultations in the hospital.

Let me backup, the lockdown news came on a weekend, the third weekend of March. There was not much clarity regarding what was going on, or at least not from what I can remember. Many of my siblings, who are also physicians, were getting a paper from the hospitals we were on staff for to show police if we get stopped – to prove we were supposed to be going places to work, that we are an essential worker. I was now carrying my work identification with me everywhere, thinking the police were going to stop me. Of course, it wasn't like that at all. Again, there was not much clarity in all the decisions made during the beginning of lockdown, such as no one coming or going.

The world was in chaos.

People were getting really anxious and nervous.

Fear.

I feel like any crisis in human life either brings out the best or the worst of people. You will see wonderful people. I remember being in line at some of the grocery stores and paying for somebody who had a few items and was in a hurry and others who were pushing and shoving. That did not help much with the contact avoidance needed to prevent transmission of the coronavirus from person to person. At that point, though, there was not much by way of official recommendation in regard to contact, masking, cleaning, and all that – we didn't have a clue as to what was best. In some issues, we still aren't completely sure what is best.

All people could think of was how they were going to be locked in their house for who knows how long, and that they needed to have enough food and supplies. For some reason, toilet paper became the hot item in all the grocery stores. Hoarding happened. Price jacking was inevitable. And, as I said, a crisis of any kind will bring the best or the worst out – and this situation was a perfect example. This wasn't just individual people. Greedy companies saw the opportunity to make an extra buck, instead of an opportunity to be supportive as part of a solution in what was unfolding as a big crisis.

We covered our faces in desperation, for we didn't know what came next.
No one knew from one minute to the next what was going on.

The mass confusion came.

People were not sure this could ever happen to America. We were hearing the news that yes there is this coronavirus in other parts of the world, but we thought that we were immune. We truly did. My doctor friends in other countries were envious of us in America, knowing we would tackle the problem before it starts. After all, we are America.

We're the first one who walked on the moon. We're the one who changed the results of any war in any part of the world.

We are the power of the world.

The virus should be ashamed of trying to get to us, the American people. People had so much trust in the system and they went on with their life. Under this time with COVID-19, we saw some of this crumble, in great part to the insurance company recommending horrible plans to patients who don't learn it was horrible until in the midst of seeking expensive medicine or procedures. That and the medical industry was not prepared for this virus to arrive in America. When the lockdown happened, the hospitals were not prepared.

By the end of March, early April, the wave of patients coming into the already busy emergency rooms exceeded the ability of the staff to handle most emergency rooms in Community and University Hospitals. I just kept thinking about how it would have been so easy to have been prepared, even if just a little more prepared.

At that point, my main thought was that for years we had been talking about the nuclear wars we had been trying to prevent all over the world, as well as the search for nuclear weapons. For years, we'd been thinking about nuclear weapons, all our life. Probably since 1945, when the first atomic bomb was dropped. We've been in negotiation with North Korea. We started wars in many parts of the world, in the name of stopping nuclear weapons. For this, you would think that we would be prepared for a medical emergency, as a nuclear weapon would cause this. It's on our mind and being prepared for a nuclear war, meaning you have a plan and the plan should be a universal isolation system, a command system, and a plan to be able to help the people affected by nuclear fallout. Meaning, a system should have been in place for a grand emergency that spanned the whole of society – one that required quarantine.

Beyond the political and military aspects of war, we had nothing in place – no medical plan.

At least, we should have had an alert in place. I mean, they train medical professionals to triage, to code – code blue, code red, code green, code black. Those codes refer to different kinds of issues, such as weather, terrorist, abduction, and, of course, patients being near collapse or already there. We have codes for every single emergency. For fire. For earthquakes. In any hospital, in any big community, in small communities, hospitals prepare for those singular events, yes, but so does every school, every college, many businesses. It seems, though, that no one ever thought about training us for the actual nuclear fallout, or a virus outbreak, both of which would be anything but a singular event.

That is basically what we were and have been dealing with in regard to COVID-19. It is no different than nuclear fallout, right down to the confusion over everything from healthcare to life in general. The virus is definitely contagious, but so is the after effect of the fallout, personally, professionally, economically. This coronavirus issue is so widespread and so scary to a lot of people that it is as if a nuclear bomb has exploded and the fallout is contaminating life as we know it.

We knew it could come, yet we were not prepared for it.

This is when the confusion happened.

Decisions.

Anybody who's in power started making decisions, sometimes seemingly for the effect of appearing to do something, anything. The number one worst decision, in my opinion, was to not let in the family members of patients, regardless if they were diagnosed with or suspected to have COVID-19, or simply had other issues. If they were in the emergency room, they were all alone. If they were in the hospital, they were all alone. No one with them. This carried a negative impact throughout the life of so many people, not only patients and the family members, but the doctors, nurses, and other staff members too.

Basically, here's what was happening:

You suspect a family member of having the coronavirus.

You put them in a car.

You drop them off – and you stay outside.

At that moment in the early stage of the disease, there wasn't a lot of talk about masks. We were still not even sure if the virus was airborne, or droplet transmitted, or some other way of transmission. Even now, it is still that scary monster which we cannot see and we don't know what it's capable of.

This monster had reached our shore in America. Obviously, they were strong, they were not afraid of us. We should have been better prepared. All we had was a plan to isolate, leaving people all alone.

Here was the recommendation, you bring your family member in a car, keep the windows open and the air flowing in the car, and drop them at the emergency room. Here they were in the emergency room alone, scared, not knowing what the next step was going to be. Not knowing if they're going to be the number 100 or 101 case or death, depending on what was being counted in a given moment. In these cases that have been reported on a regular basis, they would get admitted. They may not have been admitted on the same day. They may have stayed in the emergency room hallway alone, having not been assigned a room for quite a long time.

In the old days, we would get annoyed with so many family members as we dealt with patients in the hospital. In reality, family members were, and are, an important part of treating any patient, not only giving them support. They also provide patients with a lifeline that you know that we're here and we care about you. They help the medical professionals look at things.

Many times, I remember that working in the emergency room, a family member would come and tell me that something had maybe changed with their loved one – such as their color is different. Or they're breathing heavily and they're having a new issue. They were our extra eyes, looking at the patient when we couldn't be with them all of the time. Now, we lost that. Because we were scared. We didn't know what was going to happen, if the family member was going to bring us disease, or if we were going to bring the disease to the family member. Still confused about exactly what was happening, we let the fear drive the decision: no family member allowed anywhere in the hospital or in the emergency room, even if the patient was coming for a non-COVID-19 issue.

I am not generalizing. I would say this happened in most of the hospitals, especially in large hospitals. Subsequently, many patients died either on the floor or in the intensive care or in the emergency room. They died alone, completely alone. Maybe some didn't have to die alone. Maybe having the family there would have made no difference – other than the patient not being alone. In some cases, those extra eyes could have been the difference between life and death. There is no way to know for sure.

The staff were so busy, they couldn't even reach out to the family and talk to them about what was going on. Later on, a lot of hospitals began to connect with the family through some kind of digital form. Even with video calls, it was not the same as being there. It is not the same. Many patients would get transferred back into the intensive care, intubated, only to die alone.

This was the worst time ever, in regard to human connection. I mean, even during war people didn't usually die alone. The one who didn't have friends or family in the military or in the war zone, they had someone, like some stranger would be there to hold their hand, to get their last word to their loved one, to have them take their last letters and deliver them somehow to whomever. It is important that in the worst time of a person's life they have someone present with them, whether they survive or die. It may very well change the outcome.

This aspect of the loss of the human connection really was the main reason why I started thinking about just how unprepared we are for an outbreak such as COVID-19. It is more than this, though. This confusion and the decision about not allowing anyone in I viewed as a bad decision. Yes, it was unprecedented times, and we didn't know the impact, but leaving people alone, well that just wasn't right. Once we started to see this, we needed to revisit this ruling, like we need to do with all major decisions on a regular basis, to ensure that we are doing the right thing, to do no harm.

In my life, running a practice and even taking care of people, I revisit decisions, reassess. Constantly. Sometimes, nothing changes. Sometimes, a lot changes. Not this decision from the higher-ups – a month later, still the same story. No reconsideration, just, no family allowed. Three months later, if the patient was dying then the family was allowed, maybe... one at a time. Maybe.

This was the only change made early on. Down the road, probably three to four months into this whole situation they shifted the decision about allowing a patient's family in up to the nurse and doctor responsible for patient care. The nurse really was the main deciding factor because nurses truly were in the front line more.

Of course, there were many types of decisions beyond just allowing families in. A physician would make the decision to begin treatment and it was the nurses who carried out the orders. The nurses were in the room. They were on the front line. On the front line, sometimes healthcare providers are in great danger, especially when they are trying to intubate the patients. That was one of the closest ways a physician would get to a major exposure to the virus. The nurses, they were there, up close and personal. Day and night, in it with the patient, suctioning the tubes, administering medicine.

All the decisions about family members being let in were left to the nurses, as it would impact them most directly. From time to time, a physician had something to say, but it was mainly the nurses who would permit a family member to go in and stay with the patient. Often, only one person though, and they would be the one to initiate digital connection with the rest of the family.

It was the fear from the family member and the fear for the family member that led to the rule to deny entry. That, and the fear for the patients led them to make such a poorly advised decision in a time where there was great uncertainty. As with anything we do in life, we have to weigh the benefits versus the risk, including this situation. If you stay with your loved one, you will be exposed and face a greater chance of contracting the virus. To me, I would have rather someone tell me, "Here's the risk of getting sick. Here's the equipment we must ask you to use or you can get your own, and then you can be with your family member."

Educate and let the family member decide what they want. As long as it's not going to interfere with the care of the patient, they're not going to be a burden on the staff.

Personal Protective Equipment.

Of course, the lack of the personalized protection equipment was perceived as an issue right away. After the first two or three weeks we still had enough masks and gowns and gloves. As we moved further into the pandemic, we realized that the virus was not going to disappear anytime soon. It was here to stay, at least for a couple of seasons of our lives. People started to panic and horde equipment. In the beginning, most hospitals seemed fine in supplies but after the first two months, we started to worry a bit.

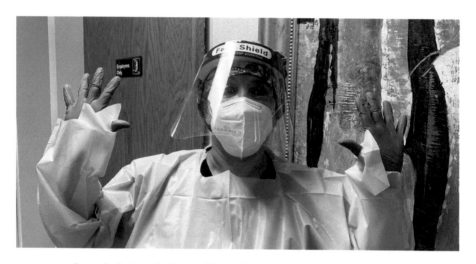

I was decked out in Personal Protective Equipment (PPE), prepared to see a patient with COVID-19. Some were not so prepared.

I had one of my patients who called because she suspected her mother had COVID-19. She asked, "What should I do? I don't live with her. And I don't have any protection."

I told her to improvise.

We used a couple of garbage bags as a gown when we needed to protect ourselves. She made her mask from a bandana. Officials were on television showing people how to make simple masks. I showed her how to do the face shields because they were not available at that time due to people taking advantage of the situation by hoarding and then price gouging. That is, they resold them with a much higher price later.

Of course, when my patient called, we were still in the early stages of the pandemic, and we just knew there wasn't any personalized protection equipment available. This patient's homemade personalized protection equipment was effective so she could be there for her mother. My patient never became sick. And her mother was not alone.

I just wish families were given options – were made part of the decision. This reality will forever haunt me, all the lives we lost, leaving them alone, scared, vulnerable.

Children.

What is worse, even kids were left alone.

The coronavirus did not hit a lot of children, but there were a few. Thirteen- and fourteen-year-old kids who had some underlying disease, such as diabetes or sickle cell anemia. These kids contracted the virus and became sick. Some died. They died alone – their lower immunity system made them more susceptible not from COVID-19 but from the underlying disease impacted by COVID-19. None of that matters really – what matters is that they died alone. They died alone. Kids died alone. They didn't have to.

Communication Barriers.

The fear and the anxiety of the illness and the unknown by itself is horrific for a patient, but being alone in an isolated room probably would kill a person even before the coronavirus forced this reality into the healthcare system. We learned later on how the virus was certainly not an equalizer, even though it does not discriminate in who can contract it. Many underrepresented populations and non-English speaking patients were impacted most drastically.

The patient who did not speak English could not communicate. Every hospital is obligated to have a translation service available, either by a person or via digital media. In-person translators were not always available after hours or at night when people were struggling, and devices don't always provide accurate translations. These patients would end up dying alone having not been able to communicate their needs due to language issues.

Most of the time, Spanish speaking patients did not have a problem. It varies from hospital to hospital, of course, but often a hospital has between 10% and 30% of the staff who speak Spanish, even during the times when translators are more difficult to find. These staff members were able to assist with Spanish translations as needed, which meant these patients could communicate their needs, even if left alone much of the time.

By contrast, the Arabic language presented a different story. Only a few communities, such as on the south side, had a few working physicians and healthcare workers who spoke Arabic and were able to help with translations. On the top of all this isolation, the sickness, the pain, the suffering, the feeling of suffocation, they were not able to communicate – and this means needs likely not being met. We are talking here about patients who were not intubated as well as those that were. With intubated patients, we used to communicate with them via writing if they were awake. They would write something for us and then we would communicate through that. If no one is available to translate, even this becomes not possible. They cannot express their needs, their pains, or anything really. If a family member could have been there, they would have served as translator.

This being alone simply was not a logical solution even with the risk of contracting COVID-19.

Six Months In.

At almost five months into the pandemic, we were feeling sorry, feeling bad about all the people who died alone. Yet, there was no revision of the visitation policy.

At least, by this time, they changed course on another matter and started allowing non-COVID-19 patients into the hospitals and emergency rooms for treatment of other health issues. They realized that closing all the hospitals and delaying care for other diseases would cause great consequences – disease was not going to take a break. A disease is not smart enough to know that we, as doctors and citizens, were busy with the coronavirus. They don't know to stop the cancer or the heart attack. The disease doesn't go on hold for a few months to give the doctors time to work on stopping the coronavirus. On the contrary, the stress of losing the job, the loved ones, the fear of getting sick, created more stress. This increased incidences of illness and made whatever condition they had worse, proving that illness was not going to stop for COVID-19. No, they wouldn't.

Everything was still happening right alongside COVID-19 and the shutdown and the dying alone. Six months in and we were just then starting to talk about the harm caused to patients by closing the healthcare system to non-COVID-19 illnesses. Six months of different kinds of diseases left untreated. Six months of morbidity increases from other diseases, bumped up against the coronavirus. They existed, of course. That's why we have so many hospitals, so many physicians. We have them because diseases are everywhere. Six months focusing on one disease alone was not going to cure any of these other diseases, not temporarily or permanently. Ignoring them for the coronavirus was an unrealistic path that created delay in care and a lot of consequences for many patients.

When hospitals started opening for other illnesses, they began to realize that maybe the family can stay with the ones who didn't have the coronavirus. Permission was granted to family members of the patients who were admitted without COVID-19. They were allowed this under one condition: they were tested for the virus. This gave the staff and the family members some assurance for safety. When they tested negative, they were able to get their procedures, be admitted to the hospital, and get the care they needed for their illness without focus on the coronavirus.

We were a step closer to normalizing how we deal with disease.

Delay in Care.

Unfortunately, a lot of patients made the choice to postpone aspects of their own care. While many hospitals did not close their emergency room to other illnesses, a lot of people decided not to go to the hospital to see what was wrong with them because of fear. They figured whatever they had was better to deal with than going to the hospital and risk catching the coronavirus. This combined with the hospitals and doctors' offices that closed their doors, meant that people simply did not receive care, whether by their choice or someone else's.

The consequences of this may take a long while to sort out, especially for some patients with serious illnesses and needed treatment, but who had their treatment delayed significantly. This included cancer patients who were on the way to get their chemotherapy and they decided, "No, I'm not going to get my chemo right now."

For a cancer patient, chemo is very, very important to get on a rigid schedule. Timing is key as when we treat with chemotherapy, we take into consideration the life of the cell. There are different stages in the life of the cell. We give one course and then in 12 weeks or so, a new cell might be regenerated and that will be the time to start another round of chemo. We killed the bad cells (and some good cells) during the first round. The newly generated bad cells will be present in blood and that will be the time to treat with another round of chemo. The timing has to be right, or it doesn't work. A lot of patients did not do the chemo, leaving at least a four- to five-month gap in treatment. Lack of treatment means less chance of survival.

For those who were in the end of life stage for their disease, cancer or otherwise, they were supposed to enter hospice. They were supposed to get comfort care – comfort care, meaning not suffering, not struggling. Being provided relief of pain, while surrounded by loved ones. This did not happen during this period. Many of these people died alone.

One of my colleagues put it in a nice way. He said the loneliest place on earth is the hospital, which is true. When you are happy you can be alone. When you're in a good place in your life and you're healthy, you can be alone. When you're sick, when you're sad, when you're nervous, when you're anxious, you don't want to be alone. Really, you shouldn't be alone. In the hospital setting, all of the above unpleasant feelings apply and that is why we should not be alone when in the hospital, even in the face of a great illness such as COVID-19.

We really did it wrong.

We owe it to a lot of the patients who died alone to revisit our policies and change them, try to make it better for whatever and whoever comes next. We need to reflect on what we have done and how much of that is going to hurt us and hurt our patients. As it is, the mistrust in the healthcare system is huge in many communities; we made it worse through our choice of action, or inaction.

Yes, you read that right: we made it worse – for everyone.

These choices made in this time of crisis without a real plan will forever change the relationship between patients and medical staff, healthcare workers and hospitals. Think about it another way. Think about your bank account or your emergency fund. You plan for your rainy days. You plan for your sick days, for your lonely days. You plan financially for the worst days of your life, which is most likely being sick in the hospital. With the money handled by your emergency fund, that worst day is not so bad from a financial perspective. That isn't the whole of the matter; there is an emotional toll that must also be paid.

We all have an emotional bank that we build up as we go through life with our friendships and family being there for each other. In this case, emotions are equitable to money. When you are able to latch onto your relationships, have your loved ones present, have your friends nearby, and have people you care about care about you, you are depositing into your emotional bank. Your emotional emergency fund is strong and you can thrive. When illness hits, the emotional bank is full and ready to be utilized. Unfortunately, patients were all alone in the hospital, denied access to their emotional bank, even as it sat full. They had no support since they could not access their emotional bank - it is almost like going bankrupt. Without it one would have a greater likelihood not to heal, because being alone becomes the stressor that brings on the worst-case scenario.

Forcing people to be alone to heal or die were the decisions made during this horrible pandemic. I will forever remember the people who died alone in a time we didn't plan for emergencies, in a time we didn't have a metaphorical emergency fund for the healthcare system but should have, in a time we didn't allow patients to replenish their emotional banks.

Ultimately, we changed the basics of human relationships altogether and the consequences were dire.

What a Mess.

It was sad to be so poorly prepared for a problem such as this pandemic. Maybe we will learn from all of this, creating a better plan for similar situations that may arise in the future. Maybe our society can have a different way to prepare for the next COVID-19 type situation, or even the fallout from an actual nuclear war.

What bothered me the most about all of this is that we just kept saying numbers; a lot of patients simply became numbers. They kept referring to the number of deaths, which had increased by two more the last half an hour or three more. It was all about the numbers without realizing that they were people who died, whether from coronavirus or something else. As we reported, and still report, those numbers we forgot the humanity behind the numbers. They were someone's partner, someone's parent, someone's friend, someone's child. A person died, and in many ways the loss of this person took a village with them. Or at at the very least gravely impacted the village. I don't necessarily mean to take them physically. They created a scar on all the people around them. A scar will never be cured one hundred percent – the loss was great, made worse by the fact that they were in the hospital dying alone.

I know it's important to keep track of the numbers for statistics and the health of the community and keeping track, but literally counting and announcing those numbers were a real bother as it took away from the truth of it all. Saying this makes it all look trivial when you put it in the form of just a number. It was not trivial. It was by no means trivial.

The impact of this virus left chaos and confusion in its wake, as it embedded itself in so many people's lives, spread across a community. As human beings, we sought out comfort wherever we could, even in the form of a common children's toy: teddy bears ready for the pandemic.

A closed retail store in an airport somewhere in America.

The Closing

——◆——

During April 2020, the emergency rooms at most hospitals were swarmed with patients and already the decision had been made: No family members. The emergency room looked in some locations like a war zone. A lot of people wearing protective gear where you could not even recognize anybody and they were almost like a bunch of robots walking around.There was no human touch, no human expression, just protective gear. Sick patients everywhere. No family members; anxiety, anger, sadness. Basically, no pleasant feelings during the first few weeks of the disease.

Worst of all, the unknown.

The unknown of what was going to come next, the unknown of whether or not we were going to have enough medicine, enough beds, enough protective gear to deal with the situation for the long haul, the unknown of whether or not we were going to have enough staff. By the end of March, every state had requested all their physicians to report to a special helpline, just in case they were short in one place more than the others – this way everyone could pitch in where they were needed most. Although some doctors were not on staff in a specific hospital, they would be sent to where needed.

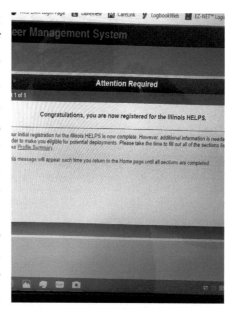

Healthcare professionals, including myself, received a confirmation like this one once they had registered to serve as needed to treat patients during the COVID-19 Pandemic.

Once registered on the helpline, documentation was sent to doctors noting that we were in the registry and we might be called for service anywhere in the state. I was prepared for the worst case, even as I had a practice to manage.

Festive Halloween decorations in my office not meant to frighten, because the virus is scary enough.

My Practice.

We closed our offices early, even before they instituted the lockdown. Staff members and close family members were becoming ill with symptoms typical for COVID-19, so they were tested. Of course, then the results wouldn't come for ten to fourteen days. They were quarantined while we waited on the results, one way or another. Due to lack of staff, a few days after testing, we had to close the office March 20. At that point with not knowing a lot about the virus, we thought it would be safer to close the office to seeing patients physically; we still kept the services open to complete behind-the-scenes tasks, such as sending prescriptions, calling with lab results, answering phone messages, and talking to panicky patients via phone and later video. We started doing telemedicine for a while, which wasn't preferred because there is an irreplaceable human touch to the practice of medicine.

36

I feel like half of medical care is a human interaction while the other half is the factual aspect of medicine and science. Despite my dislike of telemedicine, I did it because I felt that regardless of getting paid for it or not, I had to do it – for my patients who needed the continuity of care, even if altered care. The anxiety and panic for a lot of my patients was much higher than for us physicians. We ended up doing a lot of phone calls every single day. Half of the phone conversations were simply answering questions about the coronavirus, what we knew at that time, what we needed the patient to do. The other half was trying to figure out any issues with their health regarding blood sugar or thyroid levels or some other endocrine problem. We had to ensure they had their needs were met since we didn't know how long the closures would last.

Meanwhile, by the end of March, the American Association of Clinical Endocrinologists (AACE) and the American Diabetes Association (ADA) put out a statement about diabetes and the coronavirus. Although we didn't know much, we knew it was going to be worse for our patients with diabetes. We wanted to pass along to patients the messages from those medical organizations creating guidelines for protection from this disease with regard to their illness. We also wanted to talk to patients about emergency readiness for all of our patients with diabetes. Even before the official lockdown, we wanted to make sure all our patients had enough medicine for several months. They had conditions for which we could not delay treatment without grave consequences. In my practice, we recognized this; not all practices did.

Under lockdown, it was important to keep talking to our patients through telemedicine. The general population was in a state of panic and a lot of people were scared to even go to the grocery store for necessary supplies. I recognized that many of my patients live alone. I was worried about them getting enough healthy meals to survive daily life without damage to their health due to their conditions. I was able to have a catering service send some warm meals suited for patients with diabetes to some of the ones who I knew were all alone. I called them to follow up and many of them told me how their neighbors and some charities were reaching out to them already. They were getting help from good people who brought them their groceries and warm food. It was really heartwarming to see this happening in the cold environment of this pandemic. While I know it wasn't universal, I smiled at this evidence that people still cared for each other.

We started thinking about reopening the office because we felt that we really needed to see our patients face-to-face, as delaying care for anything is not a good idea. Also, we had so many new patients, it was hard to do telemedicine. In person, I have this uncanny ability to make a diagnosis within the first minute I see the patient. Being able to physically see them, I can just observe what is going on and at least 70% of the time I get it right just by looking at them. As soon as I hear their story, I think I will be right 90% of the time. When I conduct a formal examination and get a blood test, I will be right 99% of the time.

I lost all this because I could not see them, and I could not order labs for them. They were afraid to go to the lab, they were afraid that they were going to catch the coronavirus if they went anywhere. This caused a delay in taking care of patients. We did the best we could by continuing to call the patients on the schedule to check in on them and see if they needed anything, even if we didn't know them yet. We felt we had to take care of whatever we could until we could open the office physically to see patients in person. The office remained closed to in-person visits for one month, but during this one month we were on the phone constantly doing either telemedicine or even just chit chatting with the patients, calming them down and answering questions. I think I was on the phone more that month than I normally am in an entire year.

Meanwhile, we received a phone call to start going to the hospital to assist. My practice partners, who used to see the patients in the hospital, got sick early. The hospitals were becoming overwhelmed and needed more available physicians. It was already a difficult time with coworkers out sick with COVID-19 leaving me to handle phone calls and patient needs. I had all sorts of other business matters to manage to ensure we kept our practice in business, and now we were asked to help out with seeing patients as consultants in the hospital. It was a tough time in which we all worked at times twice as much as normal.

By the end of April 2020, we were able to go back to being fully staffed after being short-staffed for a significant amount of time. In May, we still had some of the sickness going on in the office, even if some could work from home. The rest of us still worked extra hours to make up for the loss of workers who simply had to stay home due to continued illness. Finally, the patients started coming back and we were happy to see them.

Safety.

It seemed like the medical offices and the hospitals were some of the safest places at this time. One of the offices I work at that is located in a hospital, had right away implemented strict screening processes, checking temperatures, giving out masks, and making sure people sanitized or washed their hands right away. We applied the same measurements in all offices, and we made sure that everybody was wearing a mask.

We came across a couple of situations in which patients did not want to wear a mask and they thought we were violating their rights, taking their freedoms away. We told them that we owe it to everybody else in the office, patients and other staff alike, to do the right thing and respect the mask policy. We had to honor the policy, no mask, no service. We referred them elsewhere, making sure the physician the patient was referred to knew the patient we were sending them had not yet received the care they needed, and if they needed anything it likely needed to be done over the phone or via video due to their issues with wearing a mask.

We tried to avoid abandonment of any patients, even when it was really their choice. We kept reminding them that as a physician when performing some operation or treatment or even when patients are sick, we are wearing masks regardless of this COVID-19 situation. In our office everybody's wearing masks, wearing shields, wearing other protective gear. While not all the time, often enough. This has been going on throughout the history of medicine.

We then remind them of the sacrifice a lot of people make even beyond healthcare, like for instance the military. Our soldiers carry heavy equipment, wear helmets, wear face coverings, and even face a need to put on a gas mask. All this has been done to protect other people. They're not only doing it for themselves and their protection, but they are doing all this work to protect other people and to keep us living the free American life.

I also reminded these patients of the construction worker who's wearing this mask all the time while helping to build the beautiful buildings and infrastructure of this wonderful country. People need to not just think about themselves; they need to think about others wearing masks making even just a small sacrifice for the goodness of all. I don't understand why a lot of people were having a hard time with the mask, beyond rare but legitimate health related problems with wearing a mask. This doesn't even account for the vast amount of mis-wearing of masks, most specifically those that had the mask under their nose, which defeats the purpose of wearing the mask. We provide them with education on the whole concept, backed up by data in cartoons or nice pictures showing how a mask lowers the chance of coming down with the infection significantly.

The least we can do for each other is wear a mask, or some other face covering. This is a simple thing that we can do for our country, rather than once again asking what our country can do for us.

By the end of May, we had the opportunity to learn from other countries. Yet, we did not do it as well as we should have. Trying to copy lessons from other countries, such as South Korea, where we knew that everybody was wearing masks. Yet, here in America, we still have some arguments in May and June and July about whether we should or shouldn't wear masks, which was frustrating to physicians. Even before the coronavirus took hold of our nation, we always had masks in the offices. When someone has a flu or cold, we try to give them the mask. In my practice, our staff would often wear masks during the flu season just to avoid the flu.

An empty waiting room, as patients were staying home to wait it out, which meant not seeking treatment.

Consequences of Delayed Care.

When we opened to patients at the end of April, we began to see the disaster of delaying the care for a lot of issues. Patients were afraid to go to the hospital, not realizing that the hospital was one of the safest places around. It was certainly safer than the grocery store, which had somebody who didn't believe in science, did not want to wear a mask before they obligated people to wear a face covering of some kind. It was difficult for people to confront those in violation of the dictate from the Illinois governor to wear a face covering in the stores. There was a lot of breaking news about retail workers getting hurt because of somebody who did not want to wear a mask.

The hospitals were already safe, as were our offices, but we still took extra measurements, such as installing glass partitions where patients now had to communicate with the front desk staff via a small gap in the window. Waiting rooms were now arranged where there would be one or two people in it. Even with wearing masks, we still tried to keep six feet apart, just in case somebody removed their mask for whatever reason. Patients were spaced now so that there would be no others waiting in the waiting room. Basically, patients would walk into our office, one at a time. After check-in they get taken directly to the exam room where they remain until their exam is complete. The room was sanitized before their appointment and would be sanitized again after their appointment.

When we are done with their care, instead of them checking out the front desk, we will bring all the papers to them in the room. They will leave through a different exit without passing by any other patients. In the rate times they pass by other people, patients or otherwise, we make sure that they both continue to have their mask worn correctly.

Meanwhile, the morale in the office was not that great. Everyone was scared still. Although many of them already had COVID-19, the fear of re-infection was high, especially with no clear data in that regard. Little by little we were seeing more and more patients, getting back into the human interaction part of medicine. Just talking to patients and comforting them was bittersweet, as we were trying to get back to some kind of normal.

At the same time, we began to hear patient stories, realizing the magnificence of the human disaster that was, no is, COVID-19. It's not only the number of deaths, of which every single one is like a whole collection of sadness, loss of deeper than a life, loss of support, loss of faith, loss of certainty. All this was associated with the loss of one of our patient's relatives, and then we began hearing about situations in nursing homes. We heard stories of a loved one who died alone, and the family will never ever forgive themselves, but there was nothing they could do.

It's unfortunate how many decisions were made without consideration to what would happen later. Medicine isn't just about preventing and treating disease, it's about people, interacting with people. Really good doctors know that if a patient has a strong support system, then even the most dire circumstances can be overcome. As noted earlier, being alone, without that support system, is not good for the health of the patient. This steals hope. Without hope, all is lost.

While we were listening to the stories of our patients, we were also seeing the number of the patients being admitted to the hospital for COVID-19 begin to slow down. We finally had a lot of protocols in place to decrease the contact for physicians without losing the human aspect. Of course, some doctors were still conducting care via telehealth or video, which the insurance companies had determined would be covered as though an in-person appointment.

I would like to step back a minute and point out that the true heroes in this whole situation were the nurses, the nurse aids, and the medical assistants. These staff members were by the patients' bedsides way more than any doctor. They were in some cases the only real human touch patients received, even at great risk to themselves. Doctors gave the orders, verbal or in writing, but it was these people that carried them out, best they could when short on staff and without a key link in the chain, the observant family member. It is these people that witnessed the vast number of disasters of patients dying alone.

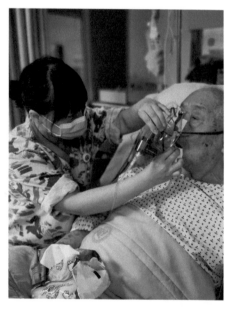

A nurse takes care of a patient, even at great risk to themself, as this is the oath they take. Truly a hero.

Moving Toward Perceived Normality.

It seems like every state got hit at a different timeline. Even with this, we still did not learn any lessons. Although Washington state was the first to have the symptoms show up, believed likely due to greater connection with China and more travel numbers from China, but soon after cases started showing up in California and New York. Then it spread to other states. When the lockdown orders started to come down from state leaders, some states delayed in issuing any restrictions.

For many Americans, there was no clarity as to what a lockdown even was. We really were making up the response as we went.

Essential workers, such as doctors like myself, were needed. So were nurses and other healthcare workers. But so were grocery workers and transport providers and police and many others. We especially cannot forget about the postal carriers... they did their job, day in and day out, with little focus on them as an essential worker. For me, I remember running to the mailman with a small gift or some food as appreciation for simply doing what needed to be done.

An essential worker providing service to keep life moving even
behind imposed COVID-19 restrictions.

In those first days of lockdown, when so many were scared to go anywhere, the postal workers and other delivery service personnel, such as Amazon or FedEx workers, were almost a hero delivering both our necessities and pleasure. They were essential and wonderful to come across as a reminder of what was once seen as normal, even if they were expected then to wear gloves and there was advice to clean your packages, both of which have since been deemed unnecessary.

In it all, no one talked about the non-essential workers now working from their residences amidst the distraction of their personal life. Or those who lost their jobs. Even if this was brought up, it wasn't really addressed. Or the teachers who had to shift their entire profession, literally over night to ensure the children received their knowledge. While there was focus on this early on, even they were assimilated into this new normal of life after the lockdown.

At least for those who decided to venture out, there was no traffic and the environment cleared up quite a bit. But at what cost? Deaths that could have been avoided. Economic destruction that could have been mitigated. And a threat for a new normal for the long haul. A world ever changed, when much of it could have been avoided if we had just been prepared, even a little bit. Hopefully, we never face a situation like this again. We need to start planning for a disaster like this now, using this pandemic as a teaching tool.

It will be easy, just write down all the things we did wrong, and then don't do it again. That way, we will have a better approach to facing COVID-19, take two.

Visitation with family took place through glass windows, if at all.

Nursing Homes

———◆———

Nursing homes are a necessary evil, at least in America. They are without question one of my least favorite concepts in America. There are not many nursing homes where I came from because you take care of your elderly, the family takes care of the elderly. I'm not going to be debating if this is right or wrong, it was just the way it was where I came from. No matter your thoughts, the nursing home is not a pleasant concept even in America.

It's almost like you are on a train throughout your life and this is your last station. There's no other station after this one. You cannot go back to another station. You cannot go forward whenever you want to.

Basically, you are waiting for something and this waiting for something is only one thing. Please indulge me as I clarify the whole idea of a nursing home, how grim the concept is. The resident of a nursing home sees the same people every day, either their other co-residents, or the staff. It's almost the same people every day. The nursing home resident lives their day according to who's coming to visit them, and when they're coming to visit them.

Their day is not divided by hours. Their days are divided by who's coming and when. My patients who live in nursing homes tell me all they do all day long is wait. That's what they wait on. To see their loved ones. Relive the life they gave to their loved ones. Remembering how they had such a wonderful time and life with their loved ones when they see them. This is the life of a nursing home resident.

It's not a general rule, but this is most of the rules of nursing homes. They're not traveling. They're not getting deeper into the meaning of life. Yes, they are reading, and they might be watching some recommended movie by the place they're living in. But there isn't much to it, this life in a nursing home.

Think about, you are in a transition. We move through life to different stages and we stop at every station at some point. There we wait until the next stage of our life. For nursing home residents, this is it. It's the holding area. It's the holding area for something that will be coming sooner or later for everyone.

Then the coronavirus happened.

A grim picture is painted with regard to COVID-19 and nursing homes. Remember, the nursing home residents were not allowed to leave. Even if they were allowed, they were not going out partying, bringing the coronavirus to their co-residents. They were just staying in their rooms and waiting on people to bring their medicine, to bring them their food. Some of them were told to stay in their room early in the stage of the disease coming to America.

Meadowbrook Manor in Willowbrook, which is right in my backyard, had the first forty coronavirus deaths in an Illinois nursing home. Most of these statistics were by mid-May. Nursing homes accounted for more than half of Illinoisan deaths from COVID-19. The Illinois Department of Public Health showed that 52% of the morbidity rate in Illinois was tied to long-term facilities, assisted living facilities, or some other kind of nursing home.

We are not just talking about the city of Chicago. In some of the down south suburbs, 70% of the coronavirus deaths were linked to nursing homes. Statewide, twenty-five nursing homes have at least twenty COVID-19 deaths each. The next highest coronavirus death was at Villa at Winter Park, which is a two hundred forty-bed facility in Chicago's South Shore neighborhood and was linked to thirty-seven fatalities. A downstate home, Villa East with one hundred nine beds had twenty-three fatalities.

There were seventeen hundred laboratory-confirmed cases that came from nursing homes. The leader of the cases came from state-owned Elisabeth Ludeman Developmental Center, which is a five hundred ten-bed facility in South Suburban Park Forest. It usually houses people with intellectual disabilities, which is a wonderful thing because a lot of younger persons with disabilities stay in that home. They had three hundred sixteen cases and ten deaths. Many of those nursing homes were privately-owned, and some of them state-owned. The worst thing was the transparency really did not exist to the family or to the resident. Most simply didn't know what was going on.

I'm giving you these numbers to show you the grim picture of the reality of nursing homes.

Family Denied.

One of my patients and her mother, who is also my patient, told me about the mother's experience at the nursing home where she lives. Mrs. S raised a large family, nine children, most of them in Illinois. They usually took turns visiting her. Sometimes, because there were nine of them, and there are seven days in the week, two of them would be together in one day, and she bragged about raising a big family. She was brought to my office by different family members almost every time because they all wanted to be involved in her care. She was smart and witty. She used

An elderly patient and their daughter. In some cases, the only way they could see each other was to go to the doctor.

to make fun of me that I only had one child. She would joke, "Well, we'll see if she's going to take care of you when you get older.

"See, I know if one of my kids moves away, or two or three or four, I still have a few more for my rainy days," she would say, and I would laugh.

I would say, "Well, I'm not planning to have anyone take care of me. I'm going to be taking care of everybody until the last day of my life."

Then, she would say, "You will see, and you will remember me."

Then the coronavirus hit, and I did not see her for a while. Her daughter also became my patient. We called a couple of times to check on the daughter and the mother, but I wasn't able to get a hold of the mother. Almost early May, the daughter made an appointment without the mother. When I saw her name on the schedule, my heart glitched. I almost felt as if there was something wrong happening.

The daughter, Lucy, came in and right before she was triaged, I walked in the room, I said please tell me your mother is okay.

She burst into tears.

It was that moment when I really decided I'm going to let their stories be heard. I had the other provider take care of other patients for a little while, as I really wanted to spend time with Lucy to learn her mother's story.

She told me how devastating everything was. She said, right at the end of March, they just got the call that nobody was allowed in the nursing home. The nursing home residents were not told what was going on, but were told it was best not to be allowed to have any visitors. At first, they let the residents roam around and go from their rooms to the dining hall and to the activity room. Then they were limited to only the dining hall, and then they made them stay in their rooms.

Imagine you're staying in a six by six room, or maybe bigger in some cases, for almost two months. They will bring you your food and they will bring you your medicine. All alone like that for months.

Mrs. S was able to talk to her family. They all spoke to her on the phone and she started to get weaker and weaker and weaker. The family kept asking to visit her. She didn't have COVID-19, but still no visits – no visits were granted. They were told no every single time.

I asked if they told the place they would sign the paper to be responsible if something happened to them. "Did you insist? Did you tell them you will wear protective gear?"

Lucy said, "Yes, yes, we did all that. And my mother was getting weaker and weaker. It's almost like she gave up. She was just tired of living like this."

It's no different than a jail. Literally, maybe a little bit better, but some jails are even fancier. Then finally, Lucy, who was the oldest, insisted and she talked to the people in charge of the nursing home. She made sure to make some point that if something happened to her mom they would be responsible. They kept telling her we're bringing the doctor in and he's checking on her. Just her heart is weak.

Finally, Lucy was able to go in. She went into the room. Her mother saw her, held her hand and she gave her this deep look, which will melt your heart if you would have seen it. Meanwhile, all the family members are calling Lucy asking, "Can we talk to mom? Can we talk to mom? You're there now? Can we talk to mom?"

Her mom then closed her eyes, and she left this world, peacefully, but with a broken heart.

Lucy was sad but she did something interesting. She asked all the family members to talk to their mother. She told them, "Mom can you hear you. She just cannot talk. She's weak. She would love to say goodbye to all of you. I'm going to put you on the phone with her and you can tell her everything you want to tell her."

Lucy said, "I will translate her reaction to you."

They started one by one, talking to their beloved, dead mother, not knowing that she was dead. They were excited, she could hear them. That's what they thought. They thought that they were telling her stories they would have never told her before. They were telling her how much they loved her, of course, they told her some of the secrets. They told her some of the things they regret. They told her that it really broke their heart not to be able to see her for the last two months. And many of them regret it, letting her go to the nursing home.

All this with Lucy sitting in the room with her dead mother, letting her eight siblings talk and talk and talk and spill their heart out to their mother thinking that she can hear them. They were happy that they were able to tell her something before she left this world. After a long talk, Lucy could not take it anymore. She told them, "I'm going to hang up now. I'm going to call the doctor. Mom is almost taking her last breath. Please let me be with her."

Lucy sobbed and sobbed and sobbed next to her mother until there were no tears to spill anymore.

Couplehood.

Mr. and Mrs. K were both in a nursing home. One of the things you might feel that will give you some comfort is staying in these dark places with the person you want to be with for the rest of your life, which is your partner, if you're lucky. Of course, they were in separate rooms.

When the news broke that the coronavirus was everywhere, they asked them not to see each other. Mr. K was having a little early dementia and he just could not take it. He would go violent and then they had to transfer him to another floor. For many of the patients who do have some kind of early dementia, being isolated may make it worse. That's what happened in his case. He was just getting worse and worse. He was moved to a floor where they would have a little bit more nursing staff to attend to the ones who were having severe dementia. He declined rapidly. He was transferred to the hospital. He acquired COVID-19 and died alone without family members, even his wife. His wife wasn't even told all the truth at the time.

The rest of the family were not allowed to go in, at the nursing home or the hospital.

I am a strong believer that the social isolation and the lack of family support especially for early or advanced dementia patients made it at least ten times worse, all because of the decision to not have a family member anywhere. It should have not been a general rule. I have already said this, but it is worth repeating, families should have been given an option to be near their loved one, to be given a choice to use protective gear and go in. The chance of getting the disease is probably higher, but their chance of letting their loved one die alone is way more than that.

Mr. K was put on the ventilator for almost ten days.

It's amazing and beautiful how a spouse leaves and another spouse will literally lose interest in life. Mrs. K was getting weaker and weaker. She did not get the coronavirus, yet she was getting worse every day, and was transferred to the hospital. She died twenty-four hours after her husband passed, and she hadn't even been told he died. I almost feel like this was an accelerated departure, for both of them, literally from the hasty decisions of isolating people, and not allowing anybody near them.

We know the value of human touch, and I know risk will be there. There's nothing wrong with touching and taking precautions and washing. We know the value of hugs. I'm not advocating hugs left and right, as I used to do in my office. I miss so much hugging many of my patients, but for the one who needed it the most when they are in despair, when they are sad, when they are weak, when they know the end is near. A hug will make it or break it for them. Many of the COVID-19 patients and non-COVID-19 patients who were nursing home residents did not get that.

We simply became isolated and computerized following the new protocols to protect against COVID-19, logging numbers in and out.

Relaxing the Rules.

One day in September while at my practice, I heard the latest nursing home story. They were relaxing their rules. They were letting residents see their families for thirty minutes a week – just thirty minutes a week – outside. Either they sat in the gazebo or they sat outside. Even if they were active, like my patient, Lydia. Lydia was 90 years old. Her ninety looked seventy and she acted so young. She had been my patient for twenty-two years. She was a nurse. She took care of her husband. She was smart. She never came to the office without a book in her hand, just in case. If she was going to wait for ten, fifteen, or thirty minutes, she would read and be a better person, as she put it. She said, "Every single page I read, I am one page smarter and one knot smarter."

She called it knot. She used to sail a lot with her husband; she was one knot smarter. And she was. She was so smart. She started coming with her daughter, and I didn't ask about it right away. Then finally I did, "Lydia, you always took care of your husband, a lot of other people. Why are you coming with your daughter? Is anything going on? Are you having memory problems?"

I talked to her daughter. I said, "Is Lydia okay?"

She said, "Yeah, yeah, she's okay."

Then I said, "I mean, not that I mind seeing you. I don't mind seeing you but just concerned that Lydia is needing help at this point of her life, which is kind of expected but I don't think it's necessary yet because she's very smart." If I ever see a need in any of my patients when they start declining, I reach out to the family myself, and I don't wait until the family calls me. I discuss the patient's social and mental status, especially if they're having some memory issue.

As you would imagine, after twenty-four years in practice, I do have a lot of elderly patients and they've been my patients for all my practicing life. With Lydia, she didn't seem to need help.

The daughter said, "Can I tell you a secret?"

I said, "Yes."

She said, "This is the only way I can spend time with my mother." She said to me, "As you can see, we're coming here almost every month. Although you keep saying she doesn't need to. She can come every three months, but we're calling and making appointments, because that's the only way we can spend time with each other."

It really broke my heart.

You really have to take your loved one to the doctor to be able to spend time with them? This woman was healthy, worked hard all her life to be at age ninety and still able to take care of herself. Now her daughter was coming to take her to the doctor just to spend time with her.

It was more than just sad, it was wrong.

When I heard this, I had them sit in my office, which I had not given my office to anyone during these COVID-19 times, because I was trying to stay away from everybody. My office was my chamber for myself only. But not that day. That day, I opened the door to them. I told her every single time she came to see me for a doctor visit, they could bring lunch and spend as long as they wanted relaxing together in my office.

Window Visiting.

Window shopping is an old concept. But window visiting is a new concept. This is what we end up doing. Window visiting with families. That's what happened in the nursing home due to the coronavirus.

My sister always says, "The noise of the family is peace to the heart."

The nursing home decision to isolate its residents steals the peace from their hearts, with devastating results.

When people moved to the nursing homes from their houses, they were promised to be able to keep their family environment, keep some semblance of the noise they knew before. That's why nursing homes had a lot of activity. They have a lot of social committees, games, movies, bingo. All those were the heart of any nursing home, just in an effort to move them safely from their home environment and the noise of the home into the nursing home. Unfortunately, the nursing home was the most hit by COVID-19 because with the indoor congregation, there were huddles of a lot of the coronavirus and it spread easily. That affected how everybody saw the nursing home situation.

Many parties were involved in making the decision about significantly locking down the residents of nursing homes until the end of June when they relaxed some of the rules, allowing them to see their family members from a distance, through a window. Of course, by then, for many it was too late.

The activities went down significantly. The interaction with a human being had been halted. That did not need to happen. Unfortunately, a lot of nursing homes were lacking enough personnel and they were lacking enough experience to deal with such a situation. The salaries were not high enough to attract highly qualified people, and unfortunately the way it should be isn't the way it was. Due to salaries, benefits, and other factors, those who care were less likely to be the ones working in this environment. Fact is, many nursing homes were established for profit and the more they squeeze out of the worker and the more they get paid from the resident (or their insurance), the more profit the nursing home pockets for their owners. A lot of greed guides the practices in many nursing homes, with the bottom line determining everything from visitation to diet.

This leaves little options for the resident. Quite frankly, video chatting, window visits, and some remote activities just will not do.

There's nothing that can replace the human touch.

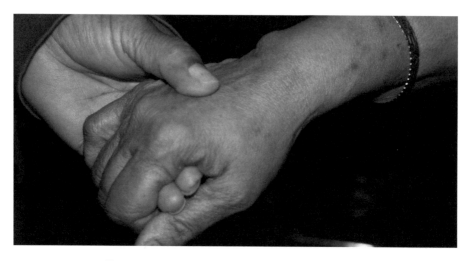

Human touch is the cornerstone of healthy interaction –
without it the distance becomes unbearable.

Strangers Among Us.

Add to all of this the reality that the people who are working in the nursing homes are wearing personal protective equipment. You cannot even see an expression, let alone a smile. You are looking for some comforting sign, you're looking for some compassion, which you cannot see in the eyes of the worker you have to trust for your wellbeing.

A lot of residents were dealing with unfamiliar faces, although they had been familiar faces at some point. When you cover with a mask the only thing showing is your eyes, and people look alike. Your favorite nurse who was there for you all the time may not be there or even if she is there, she doesn't look any different than anybody else. She cannot comfort you; she cannot smile, she cannot show her expression. She cannot hold your hand. A lot of nursing home residents become less interactive. Even later on when they were allowed to see their family outside with precautions in place, a lot of family noticed significant decline in their health, in their eagerness to live. Their mental status went down significantly, especially those with early stages of dementia. Their dementia got much, much worse.

I saw in my own practice, and many of my colleagues shared with me, the isolation triggered a lot of need for psychiatric medicine. There was a huge increase in requests for antidepressants, antipsychotics, and anxiety medicine. This was unfortunate, it was hard not to prescribe it. At the same time, it was a double-edged sword where if we didn't, they were going to suffer more, and if we did, that would deepen their isolation.

By early July, most of the nursing homes had begun to expand the controlled outdoor visitation, but the inside activity was still slow to return due to staffing issues. Unfortunately, many of the sick were staff from nursing homes. We lost a lot of healthcare workers from nursing homes due to either death or fear of going back to work. They rightfully didn't want to be exposed to the virus, but this shortage of good staff members placed greater stress on nursing homes, which increased the need to isolate residents instead of providing more personal attention, as residents needed it.

A healthcare worker ready to see a patient, decked out in personal protective equipment as became the expectation across hospitals in America.

This was especially true for those with dementia, which gets worse with isolation. We saw it get ten times worse for the patients who are living in the nursing home. They were kept in their rooms all alone, which made the situation harder. The lack of proper personal protective equipment made the conditions dire, sometimes to the point where the food was left at the door, with medication left in cups. Social hours were eliminated, and residents now lived among strangers. They were strangers even to themselves, simply because they had little to no human connection with anyone, let alone being able to see their family.

Our leaders keep emphasizing social distancing and wearing protection. However, if you have adequate personal protective equipment, you don't need the social distancing. It's pretty much like what we do in our practices, we're seeing people close to us. Outside of healthcare, when you go to the grocery store, most are not practicing six feet of distance, as there really isn't room.

The confusion was, and still is, which one should we practice? Social distancing or wearing protection?

Yes, if you were not wearing anything, it was important to make sure you were six feet apart, but when protective equipment was involved, the distance wasn't really needed. Based on this reality, supervised outdoor and indoor visits could have been done easily within the nursing homes. None of this was done. Rather they chose to push isolation as though the strangers within the homes were not that important. Ultimately, failure to thrive due to lack of contact was the main factor in the decline of many of our nursing home residents.

Healthcare workers in personal protective equipment.

Healthcare Workers

———◆———

The age of technology brought a new meaning to our health and to what we've done in our society following the birth of COVID-19. From goodbyes and farewells and funeral homes to a scheduled iPad phone call. We used technology to connect the sick in the hospital with their loved ones, we used technology to treat patients, we used technology to give medical orders, and we used technology to collect data in order to make major decisions. We've truly transformed through technology in our lives – even to the darkest days and as related to our mortality.

For healthcare workers, technology became a saving grace within the practice of medicine a bit too late for some. The stories of healthcare workers are a sad collection of reality.

Nurses.

I will start this discussion with a suicide, a nurse's suicide. She got so overwhelmed with the flood of patients, filling up their emergency room and the hallways of the emergency room. She dealt with it for a few days, but then she could not take the pressure anymore. Not only that, there was such chaos with increasing numbers of COVID-19 patients and the virus spreading rapidly. We still didn't have clear guidelines as to how to handle the situation because it was changing so quickly, by the hour, by the minute even. Pressure was everywhere, as was the uncertainty. It was too much for her and she decided to end her life.

The nurse finished her shift and she looked at the line of patients and she decided to have an end to it. Her way. She threw herself from the seventh floor. She died at the scene and the irony was when they saw her, they called the paramedics, but the paramedics were in the emergency room already bringing patients, many of them. They tried CPR. They brought her right into the the nearby emergency room where she worked, but she did not make it.

Do you know how long it takes to make a good nurse? Nursing school is not many years. It is probably two years after college or some colleges they can do it within their college years. They will finish studies in two to four years, but it takes a long time until they are the wonderful nurses they are. They were the heroes who were following the doctors' orders, who were making sure everything was done properly.

It's them – the nurses – that I look to first.

These are the people who see the first sign of distress, who relieve the stress. It's the nurses that a patient is often more comfortable talking to, especially when the patients need to talk to someone, anyone – someone to hear them, to provide a reassuring voice when no family member is around.

Suddenly, any patient who comes through the emergency room for any reason, not necessarily COVID-19, for any other reason will not have a companion. The family member cannot be there. Even if the patient is deaf or the patient needs translation, or the patient has a disability, or the patient's just mentally unstable to be alone. That really did not matter – they were alone, all the patients who were admitted for COVID-19 or Non-COVID-19 between March 20th up until September (and beyond in some places, sooner in others), no family member, not even given a choice to get dressed up in personal protective equipment. Not told to enter at your own risk. Nope. That was not an option.

The nurses were the only people many patients could confide in and receive some compassion from.

Yes. As I said, it is only four years to make a nurse, but it takes longer, a decade, two decades, to make a compassionate, good nurse. Unfortunately, we lost a lot of them. We lost a lot of them because of COVID-19, to COVID-19. They could not say, "No, I will not go in."

They could not refuse to be a helping hand. They could not stay away. Many of them took that home with them, took it to heart. It wasn't easy to deal with all that. It was not easy. Many of these nurses entered the field because they love to help others... nurses are like this, helping others. It impacted the nurses and the healthcare industry when they were lost either due to death or simply being unable to not take the pressure anymore.

As a physician, you might think I would talk about my colleagues or myself more, but I think the heroes here were the nurses first. And us second.

I could never do their job. It is amazing what they do. When you know what the nurses do, you really have a totally different attitude to how you deal with nurses, how you evaluate nurses, how much they get paid, or more specifically how little they get paid. I mean, literally no matter how much they get paid, even in the best institution where they get paid better than others, still it's too little. There is no value to their job, to their helping hand, to their feeling toward their patients. No value at all.

Emergency Room Doctor.

I will talk about the emergency room physician who worked so hard to be where she's at. It is not easy to be an emergency room physician, not easy at all. This was the top emergency medicine doctor in a hospital in Manhattan. She tried to do her job the best she could. Her father said they knew she did it well, and yet she still contracted COVID-19. She survived without any major complications, and went back to work. Prior to this pandemic, she didn't have any mental illness, but this situation led her to being overwhelmed and so concerned about all the sick who sometimes died before they even saw the doctor.

She was a hero, and yet it became too much for her and she took her own life. She became "another casualty [of COVID-19,] just as much as anyone who has died" from the virus, according to her father. Another wonderful life lost due to this ugly virus.

The loss of a doctor is a loss of thirty years of hard work. The loss will not be easily replaced.

Dr. Lopez.

One interesting case was the case of Dr. Lopez. Dr. Lopez was a doctor who served and was the lifeline of a small area in Arizona. He served undocumented, underprivileged, and a myriad of different individuals from different walks of life. He was the one convergence point of all those individuals and all of their stories. Dr. Lopez had seen lifetimes of babies growing up to be children to be adolescence to be adults; he'd seen people grow up and known them their entire life. Dr. Lopez had always been the staple of this community because the one thing that a lot of people had in common, was they all went to the same doctor.

Of course, when COVID-19 came around, it hit that area like a brick.

Dr. Lopez did come down with COVID-19. COVID-19 is a universal thing that affects everyone. The ironic thing is that when it does lead to someone's demise, it could not be more isolating. This man who affected and touched the lives of thousands reiterates that it's who you impact while you are on this earth that matters most. He was a loving father, a great dancer, someone who was full of life, a fabulous doctor trusted by his patients.

Dr. Lopez died alone in a hospital.

The irony, however, is that as he impacted and helped thousands, on his way out, there was no one there. Like so many others, he is a testament to how isolated a COVID-19 patient can be. It's to the point where it even looks inhumane to a certain extent. If anything, many of these stories have taught us that you shouldn't have to die alone.

Physician Death.

Making a good doctor is a long project, a thirty-year project. For example, I finished medical school at age twenty-two, did four years of residency in Damascus university, followed by three years at Christ Hospital and University of Illinois, then two more years as a Fellow at Northwestern University Medical Center to be fully ready to practice as a doctor. Losing a lot of physicians will take a long time to replace. Overall, by end of May we had lost close to six hundred doctors and providers in the United States and the numbers are even higher in other countries. We may not feel the shortage now but it's definitely coming.

The number of the physicians who actually died are interesting statistics to examine.You might think the critical care physicians who are on the front line would have the greatest number of deaths, along with infectious disease specialists. They didn't. Although there were a significant number of deaths in these categories, they were less likely to die than other specialties. They were used to wearing protective gear and they were used to being close to extremely sick patients and being able to handle the possible contagious disease better than others. Similar to them were the emergency room physicians and the emergency room staff. Regardless, the respiratory therapists had high numbers too. The highest number of deaths before they closed all the dentist's offices were dentists.

Dentists always wear protective gear because they operate closer to the saliva, but due to the aerosol sprays and other devices they used, they were way more exposed than others. We saw a lot of deaths among dentists in the early stage of the pandemic, but they shut down any dentist office right away by the end of March and they only opened it for emergencies, which lowered the rate of death among dentists. Just like all our practices, they were way more protective, and they were screening patients. If there's any staff or any person who had possible COVID-19 they kept them in quarantine temporarily until they received their test results. They contacted all the patients who were in contact with them and they were told what to do as well, following the Center for Disease Control (CDC) guidelines.

The royal virus became a global reality.

The Royal Virus

———◆———

In February, Europe and other countries were testing people all over the place, even in the airport. The United States was not caught up. I think we might be cheated on with delay in reaction to the coronavirus. Many hospitals in their meetings in February were barely saying anything about the coronavirus. March 1 was when the first case came to New York Hospital. In suburban Chicago we began seeing cases the third week of March.

Retrospectively, we realized some of the patients we saw earlier probably did have COVID-19, we just didn't know to look for it. We didn't know exactly what they were having. COVID-19 seemed almost like an autoimmune disease, which means the body was attacking itself, rather than a foreign entity that has entered the body, such as a virus. It looked to me a little like killing a fly with a gun. The body was reacting hard to the virus, much more so than one would think. But it wasn't like any virus for those impacted so greatly. To them it was deadly, and like trying to hit a fly with a gun, we were missing things early on, but finally caught up. It was about how the body was reacting to this virus.

The body reacted by activating all the immune responses and subsequently there was some imbalance between different blood components and causing clotting in so many organs. A few months later we learned that a lot of the autopsies showed clotting and the obstruction of small vessels in different parts of the bodies. In simple words, usually the blood runs smoothly everywhere but with exaggerated immune response to the virus, it clots. The blood was not running smoothly. There were some obstacles in the vessels which carry the blood supply to the cell, and subsequently all this clotting was causing a morbidity situation. The most important impact was to the pulmonary system, where a lot of patients were having a hard time breathing and then were intubated. Many of them died after intubation. A few factors affected this. One was the clotting, meaning that there was no blood supply to some part of the lung and that some part of the lung was not taking in oxygen and pushing out CO_2.

The other part was that the body was still reacting to this virus and it was causing a lot of secretion, which were obstructing more of the airways. Subsequently, someone realized that changing the position when they put them downward had helped clear up a little bit of the airway and they had a better outcome in regard to getting a patient off a ventilator. However, the clotting factor disorders were figured out a little later after multiple autopsies. That's when they start using an anticoagulation, also known as a blood thinner, to keep the blood thin and decrease the process of the clotting.

Equalizer.

The royal virus infected the royal family, so we thought the virus was an equalizer. It infected the US President and the English Prime Minister. Even our beloved actor, Tom Hanks, contracted the virus. Therefore, it must be an equalizer.

However, that is not true.

Unfortunately, it impacted underrepresented populations more than Whites. African Americans had at least a four times greater impact. Latinos were higher in regard to deaths, hospitalizations, complications, and so much more. The exact cause was not 100% clear as so many factors played a role, including the disparity in access to healthcare, the jobs held, education, living arrangements, and discrimination when visiting any medical facility.

Also, with these populations there is a higher incidence of underlying diseases which increased the morbidity and mortality in general such as: diabetes, high blood pressure, obesity, lung disease, and heart disease.

Another wake up call, let us shorten this gap between people where we will be equal for all, not only for diseases, also in treatment, access to care, and living situations. We are equal, even in the eyes of this nasty virus that everyone could contract – it just impacted certain populations more than others due to underlying societal disease as compared to the medical diseases.

Coronavirus Defined.

The coronavirus impacts all body parts. We know this. So far, everyone's been talking about the respiratory symptom, meaning the lungs and breathing issues. This was the main manifestation of symptoms of the coronavirus on everyone, which starts with cough and shortness of breath. It also has generalized symptoms: fever and body ache. In this chapter, I'm going to break down the effect on everything else in the body. The most serious effects from COVID-19, after the breathing system, are the heart system and the nervous system.

The Heart System.

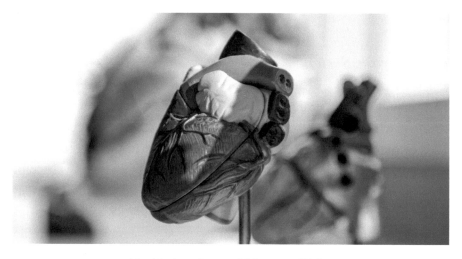

A healthy heart is essential for our wellbeing.

COVID-19 showed different manifestations on the heart, including irregular heartbeat, inflammation of the heart, heart failure, and heart attack. Many cardio symptoms, unfortunately, were silent. It usually happened when the patient had gotten worse, and they were on a ventilator. That's why a lot of patients did not manifest the regular signs and symptoms of heart issues in general. Heart-related issues were probably the second co-morbidity factor for patients who died from coronavirus. We will see the effect on the heart for years to come.

In the ones who survived the coronavirus, there is some anticipation that there is viral infection in the heart and that it weakens the heart muscle, causing an irregular heart rhythm. The ones who survived, they're being monitored closely to learn the consequences on the heart later in life. Of course, we saw a drop in the blood pressure, especially when they were having generalized sepsis where we saw irregular heartbeat from very fast to very slow. We saw poor circulation in the extremities due to clots, and possibly losing the extremities due to no circulation.

In summary, the effect on the heart was as devastating as the impact on the lung system. It simply didn't manifest in the regular way, where it would be obvious to us that it was having an impact on the heart – at least this was the case in the early stage of the virus being present in the world.

The Nervous System.

The second serious issue from the coronavirus was on the nerve and brain system. From the beginning, the nerve and brain system showed a lot of manifestations such as headache, change in the mental status, delirium, and confusion. Subsequently, we learned that there were a lot of strokes, but the same thing happened here that they did not present in the usual presentation of a stroke. Unfortunately, we learned a lot from the autopsies which showed there were significant increases in the clotting, meaning that blood was not running smoothly through all the arteries and veins. That led to a clogging in some of the brain arteries and caused stroke. That led to clots being thrown off to different parts of the brain.

Many of the patients who were admitted to the hospitals had significant confusion, mental status changes, and delirium. A few of them were diagnosed with something called encephalopathy, which is a medical term for inflammation of the brain cells. The image we usually use to diagnose a lot of mental status changes and nerve system manifestation were not utilized, due to the limitation of being on a ventilator, or due to COVID-19 itself. However, there has been, of course, a lot of emphasis and a lot of work has been put in doing autopsies to learn as much as we can from the unfortunate loss of lives. What we have seen through these efforts is that there is some viral load in the brain cell but not a lot. It was almost an indirect effect of the virus on the brain.

We also saw peripheral nervous system involvement. A lot of patients were having nerve damage. The ones who recovered were still having some nerve damage issues, some weakness, and some numbness. We also saw some rare, reactive nerve disease. It's called Guillain-Barré syndrome, which is a disease effecting neuro muscular connection. This causes muscle weakness and nerve damage, and subsequently worsens the bleeding. This is an issue in patients with coronavirus.

The Kidney.

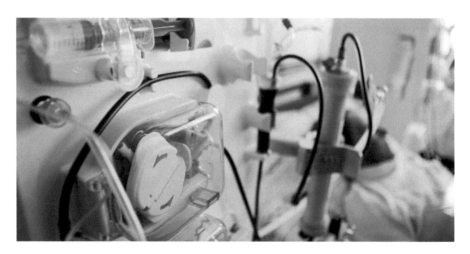

A hemodialysis machine, with bloodline tubes, become a life saving
tool for many who suffered kidney failure due to COVID-19.

With the kidney, we also saw a lot of presentations of acute kidney disease and patients needed to be on dialysis. The number of patients who needed to be in dialysis were doubled or tripled in the ones who were admitted to ICU with COVID-19 versus being in an ICU with non-COVID-19. Kidney function declined significantly, especially when the sepsis became generalized in many of those patients. We call it organ failure when they get to that stage when many of their organs stop working properly, including the kidney, and that's why many of them require medical intervention.

There was a significant shortage of dialysis chairs. The data says chairs are usually utilized for a few hours, at least three times a week, and many of the large hospitals that were hit hard had a shortage. Thanks to the cooperative system between states, there was an ability to shift many dialysis chairs to needed areas. Also, regular dialysis treatment is different from dialysis for those with COVID-19. Under these circumstances, patients needed a much more prolonged protocol. Then it was followed by greater sanitizing and cleaning. Thankfully, many of the patients who required dialysis during the acute illness of COVID-19 completed their dialysis and their kidney function recovered within one or two weeks.

Tumors and COVID-19.

Patients who have cancer, in general, and those who have received chemotherapy for cancer, are immuno-compromised, meaning that their body does not fight infection like others who are not immuno-compromised. Those who were in the act of receiving chemotherapy were much more vulnerable to the virus than others. However, conflicting data exists about the ones who survived cancer and were not on chemotherapy any longer. According to one study, even though they survived cancer within the year they were at higher risk for acquiring COVID-19 and they became sicker than others when they contracted the virus.

The reason for that mainly has to do with their vulnerability to infection in general. Although they were done with chemotherapy, many of them were on some kind of treatment that may have an effect on their immune system. A lot of places have been conducting studies to weed out the effect of cancer on COVID-19, which will tell as necessary information once those studies are released.

The other part was the interruption to the treatment of cancer, which was highly significant, unfortunately. Sometimes this was due to lack of access to medical facilities during this time. Usually it was caused by patients putting off their care for cancer for a few months, and that significantly impacted the percentage of those surviving and the cure rate. It is still too early in the pandemic to know how bad the delay of cancer treatment affected the general number and it will remain to be seen what the effect will be down the road.

Eye Disease.

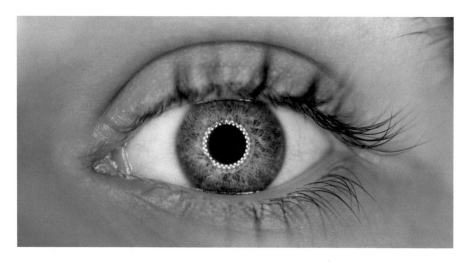

They say the eyes are the window to the soul. From a medical perspective, they are another point of transmission and are a possible window to illness.

There is a condition called conjunctivitis, where the eyes get red and discharge seeps from the corners. Unfortunately, we have learned that the eye is one more source of transmission because of the story of the eye doctor who died from COVID-19. He was the first one to alert the world one more way the virus is transmitted – through the eye. One of the important things that came of this is that people should not touch their eyes or their face. Another important way to protect ourselves from the virus became either wearing protective goggles or a facial shield.

The eye is another source of entrance to the body and it was clear early in the stage of the disease that we should not allow this access to the virus. Many of those in close contact with people were asked to either wear glasses, goggles, or the facial shield.

Ear, Nose, and Throat (ENT).

The novel coronavirus did affect otorhinolaryngology, which are head, neck, and throat disorders, as part of the ENT system. It should be noted that the respiratory system is not part of the ENT system. One of the first things noticed is the acute loss of smell and taste. And of course, the upper respiratory tract system will be included in this ear, nose, throat part where a lot of patients were having runny nose, sneeze, and sore throat. This was common in most of the patients who presented to the hospital a few days before the exacerbation of the disease with these minor symptoms, which overlap with the general flu symptoms.

The loss of smell had happened in almost 70% of the patients. For most of them their smell came back within seven to ten days from recovering. The loss of smell is extremely important. That will also affect taste and that can affect quality of life significantly. In reality, we really don't have any treatment for the loss of smell (or taste). There aren't many diseases we deal with which cause a loss

Loss of smell (and taste) are two symptoms of COVID-19. Without the sense of smell, we cannot smell the roses.

74

of smell. It was interesting to be faced with this kind of issue with a patient who had coronavirus. We have yet to learn what we can do to help patients who have lost their smell down the road.

Children and COVID.

Less than 6% of COVID cases have occurred in children. This statistic was done before the school openings, so I'm almost positive, the numbers would be a little different after the school openings. The numbers of cases and the statistics are constantly

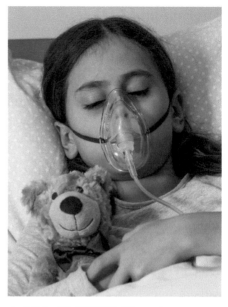

A child with COVID-19 receives oxygen from a mask and comfort from her bear, as she likely was alone in the hospital.

changing significantly. Anyway, and we know that school age children are way, way more likely to contract COVID-19 than the younger ones who are staying at home. It's interesting that the pediatric population will be the one to remember the COVID-19 epidemic the most when they seem to have the least impact and suffering from it. Hopefully, many of them will be able to get the vaccine.

There was a case where a woman gave birth to a child while positive for COVID-19. The child was, of course, separated from their mother. Many limitations were put on breastfeeding due to that. Many children have lost either parents or grandparents, which is a huge loss to the children. There have been so many studies showing that children who grow up with grandparents do way better in life than the ones who didn't. Unfortunately, the pandemic made many of our children lose their safe warm lap that they used to go to when they were sad, or when they were in trouble with their parents.

Thyroid and COVID-19.

After a few months of follow up on patients with pre-existing thyroid condition we found that they were not at higher risk. Few studies showed the patients who were admitted to the intensive care unit with COVID-19 developed some form of thyroiditis, just like any severe illness from a virus. Some of these thyroiditis forms were acute and severe forms, requiring steroids, which became the standard of care for this acute form of COVID-19 infection. Just like any other organ with large numbers of these receptors called angiotensin converting enzyme receptors 2, which almost grant an access to the virus into the tissues.

We will have to wait and see if the acute thyroiditis from COVID-19 will cause longer term effects in the future. Any patients who recovered from serious COVID-19 infections must be followed closely with frequent thyroid functions testing.

Royal Virus Doesn't Spare Anyone.

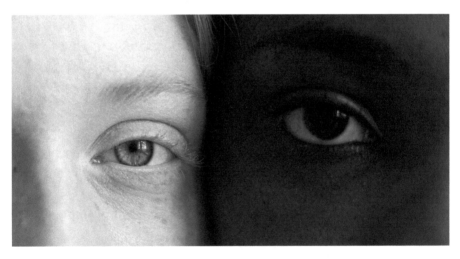

If only people saw each other as equals, just as the coronavirus sees everyone as an equal opportunity to infect.

As we can see, the coronavirus did not spare any part of the world and did not spare any part of our body. Almost every single part of the body has been affected by the coronavirus in some way or form.

Even as you are reading this book, acknowledgement must be made that we are constantly updating our knowledge on this fast moving virus, which is the nature of being still in the midst of it all, which affects us significantly.

In a few months or in a year or so, we will have way more knowledge and way more data. We can share it with the world. Luckily the scientific population and the healthcare workers are busy conducting studies and arranging for research to learn more, and to be better prepared for the next time that we hope never comes.

to **Diabetes and Coronavirus (COVID-19)**

Planning for Coronavirus

Before you get sick, make plan:

Gather your supplies:

- Phone numbers of your doctors and healthcare team, your ph
  your insurance provider
- List of medications and doses (including vitamins and supple
- Simple carbs like regular soda, honey, jam, Jell-O, hard can
  popsicles to help keep your blood sugar up if you are at risl
  too ill to eat
- If a state of emergency is declared, get extra refills on you
  so you do not have to leave the house
  — If you can't get to the pharmacy, find out about havin
  medications delivered

  ̣.ve enough insulin for the week ahead, in case

ADA statement about diabetes and COVID-19, from their website.

Diabetes and Coronavirus

———◆———

We still did not learn a lot about this disease in the first stages. I have several diabetic patients. We saw that the population with diabetes were hit way worse with COVID-19. This was probably due to the virus activating special enzymes in the pancreatic cells called angiotensin converting enzymes. That would cause the deactivation of the pancreatic cell which secretes insulin. That's why sicker patients were ones with diabetes. It was a vicious cycle. The pancreas was not working properly for these patients with diabetes, their sugar levels were increasing. They are going into a special kind of complication called diabetic ketoacidosis. The high sugar by itself was leading to exacerbate their suppression of the immune system. Thus, they were not able to fight the virus very well. In general, patients with diabetes do not fight bacteria and viruses well, but with the coronavirus it was even worse.

While people with diabetes are not at high risk to contract COVID-19 there is enough evidence that people with diabetes, especially those with poorly controlled blood sugar, are at higher risk to develop severe illness when they acquire COVID-19. They also have a much higher rate of serious complication and death than people without diabetes. Of the people hospitalized for severe COVID-19, 22.2 to 26.9% were reportedly living with diabetes.

Why patients with diabetes are at higher risk to get complications when they acquire COVID-19 because high blood sugar is linked to poor immune response to any viral infection including COVID-19 and possibly increased risk of secondary bacterial infection. Effective glycemic control can reduce the risk of serious infection and adverse outcome. COVID-19 by itself raises blood sugar. While talking about this subject, a lot of patients with diabetes have other comorbid conditions, such as weight problem, cardiovascular disease, and kidney disease, and all this increases the risk of getting severely sick from COVID-19.

We were getting so many consultations in the hospital for patients with COVID-19 and high blood sugar. Some of them were not even diagnosed with diabetes before or they were not aware of having diabetes. They were admitted with extremely high blood sugar and a complication of diabetes, which is called diabetic ketoacidosis (DKA). This where the body starts producing a lot of acetone-like products and it's a dangerous condition. It can happen in type one and type two patients, though it is rare for type two, except when an infection like COVID-19 is present. It is a condition in which patients require strict fluid control and electrolyte correction. It became quite common when patients with COVID-19 have diabetes, making it even harder to treat and to manage.

I remember when we were seeing patients in the hospitals; we kept getting consultation requests while we were making our rounds. Unfortunately, by the time we were able to see some of them, even on the same day, some of them had already died. That's when we decided to have two or three endocrinologists doing rounds at the same time to be able to manage right away the ones who were facing this serious complication. It was really sad to see that we did not even have a chance to see them due to the fast progression of the two illnesses together.

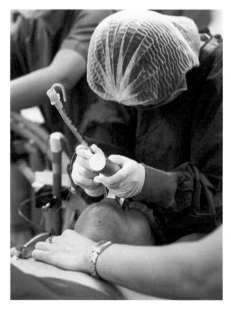

Additionally, many patients with diabetes have other comorbid conditions such as cardiovascular disease. Many of them have some underlying cardiovascular disease, which by itself increases the risk of getting seriously ill from

Doctors work to intubate a patient in an effort to save their life.

COVID-19. There is substantial cardiac damage to a lot of patients who died from COVID-19.

We have now learned a lot about the clotting system. A lot of COVID-19 patients died with clotting disorders, meaning their blood got thicker, and they grew a clot somewhere in their body. That took a while to discover. Unfortunately, there were many autopsies before we knew that the blood abnormalities were one of the reasons COVID-19 was so morbid.

All this learning process has changed our management of COVID-19 patients when they are critically ill. The coagulation and the blood thinning became one of the priorities when they got so sick like that.

The American Association of Clinical Endocrinologists (AACE).

The medical society for each field usually puts up a statement when there is any urgent need to change something regarding best practices for treatment. The American Association of Clinical Endocrinology (AACE) put out a statement about diabetes and COVID-19.

In general, COVID-19 hit individuals sixty years of age or older, and ones with pre-existing medical conditions the hardest, with diabetes at the top of the list. As I mentioned, although the study showed there is no increased risk to contract coronavirus have diabetes. However, when someone with diabetes does contract the virus, they will have worse sickness as opposed to others.

The following actions are recommended by the federal government as preparation for patients with diabetes during the COVID-19 time:

> 1. The actions for patients with diabetes will be to continue to take all their prescribed medication and that's on another notice where there's a significant shortage in getting the medication on time. That's where keeping all the offices open was important, although we were not seeing patients physically in the office,

but we definitely kept the office open for other services beside physically seeing the patient. Many patients were running out of medication. It was also important to provide samples at this time of their life more than any other time.

2. Refer to the prescriptions and be prepared for shortage of supply. We were just making sure all our patients would have at least a 90-day supply of their medications and it was important to make sure all the prescriptions were sent to the pharmacy within 90 days, and then later on if there's any refund needed to make sure to contact their provider. Many patients were getting delivery service for their medication and there were some delays in the delivery at some times. It's important to make sure they have at home that 90-day supply.

3. Stay home as much as possible to reduce the risk of being exposed. Then when going out in public to avoid crowds and limit close contact with others and avoid any non-essential travel.

4. Wash your hands with soap and water on a regular basis at least 20 seconds, which is common sense, but just more important in patients with diabetes than others. Do this especially before eating and drinking and after using any restrooms and/or blowing the nose or coughing or sneezing.

5. Cover your nose and mouth while coughing and sneezing and with the tissue and or if not available, with your inner elbow. And throw the tissue in the trash.

6. Avoid touching your eyes. It's really important this is one of the hardest things a lot of people don't realize how many times they touch their eyes. Avoid touching eyes, mouth, and nose when possible.

7. When presented with symptoms such as fever, cough, shortness of breath, or wheezing, especially if you believe you

may have been exposed to COVID-19 or live with or have recently traveled to an area of ongoing spread to call and see the healthcare professional. Immediately.

The list was a guideline for triage. After explaining the symptoms, many of them were triaged right away to either the emergency room or advised to stay home and take some precaution and they were given parameters. They were told to check their temperature to look for a fever, usually 100.4 or higher, as well as check their pulse, and their pulse oximetry. The pulse oximetry device is not cheap, but it's reasonably priced. It is actually available in most pharmacies and online. This was an important tool to help patients determine when they're getting sicker and when it is time to go to the emergency room.

Diabetic supplies are essential for life. Patients were advised to have prescriptions refilled to maintain a ninety-day supply.

On an interesting note, when a patient has low oxygen they don't feel bad. Low oxygen causes euphoria. Many patients with this euphoria were not feeling bad and that's why people were waiting too long to go to the emergency room. Meanwhile, their oxygen level was significantly low and then it dropped so much, that's when they went to the hospital. One of the things we also learned from the early stage of the disease was that they were getting to the emergency room quite late, when their oxygen went down to 70%. We want them to seek help when it gets below 90%. Patients can measure this on the pulse oximetry and get to the emergency room at a better time in their symptoms. Again, that's something we learned later on in the life of this virus.

The American Diabetes Association (ADA).

The American Diabetes Association is another provider of information available to the public on their website, diabetes.org. The ADA stated that people with diabetes face a higher chance of experiencing serious illness and death if they contract COVID-19 which is a repeat to you, I know.

However, the recent CDC data indicated that as many as 40% of the patients who have died from complications of COVID-19 had diabetes. As you can see the contrast, only 10% of the US population lives with diabetes and 40% of the deaths from COVID-19 have diabetes. This disproportionate figure is an indication of the grave risk that people with diabetes face should they contract COVID-19. The CDC declared as soon as they knew that complications from COVID-19 increase to high risk for the patient with diabetes.

In general, patients with diabetes are more likely to experience severe symptoms if they get any kind of infection. The infection gets worse when the blood sugar is above target. When it's uncontrolled, it will lead to severe complications. Another unfortunate fact is that 92% of the type two patients with diabetes are overweight. We will just have a little extra data about obesity and COVID-19 and that did not help the type two patients with diabetes.

Many patients with diabetes have heart conditions and kidney issues. Which definitely lowers their ability to fight infection significantly. The ADA also took a serious stand about individuals who have diabetes being easily accommodated due to the American Disabilities Act because they are substantially limited to any major activity in regard to their endocrine condition.

The ADA stated that the COVID-19 pandemic may affect the employees who have been working without any accommodation, and with COVID-19 they may require special accommodation right now, although many of them probably were not needing any accommodation before.

For the time being, with COVID-19, accommodations are required, such as telework, temporary assignment to meet the physical distancing recommendation, either of certain job function or another actually vacant position, temporary leave of absence, or in modification of the work environment to reduce the viral transmission, such as installing plexiglass barriers. We probably learned this as soon as all the states started to open their practices and businesses to work. Many places began putting this plexiglass and it does show some reduction in the risk.

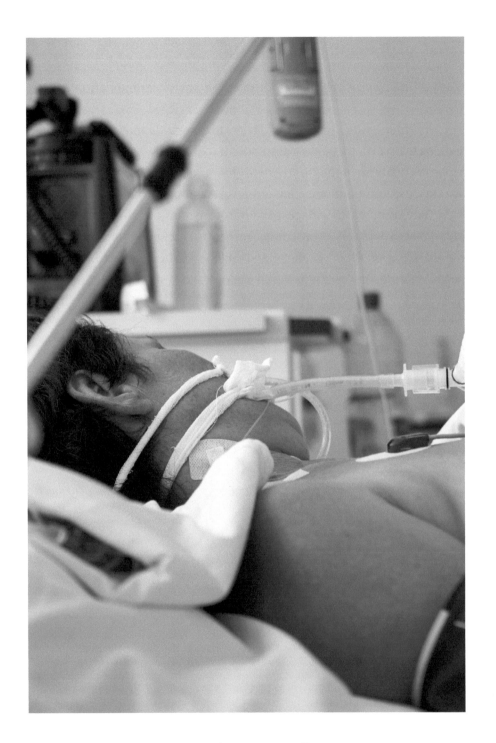

Obese patient on a ventilator.

Obesity and Coronavirus

Obesity is a serious problem in the United States.

A few weeks into the coronavirus pandemic in the United States there were a lot of younger people in intensive care; even the death rate among the younger population was much higher than any other part of the world. Looking back, it was noted that most of the younger population who died or had serious complications from COVID-19 were overweight; their Body Mass Index was above 35. The incidence of obesity is around 40% in the United States, compared to 6% in China and 20% in Italy. Because of this, we are among the highest rate of the coronavirus and death in the early stage of the disease's presence in the world, before third world countries caught up to these numbers. Yet the death among the young was much higher in the United States. They looked at the category of their Body Mass Index.

The Body Mass Index is a measurement to know how obese a patient is. In simple words, if I tell you somebody weighs 150 pounds, it doesn't mean anything. If they are five-five or taller than five-five, they're not overweight. If I tell you it's somebody who weighs one hundred fifty and they are four feet tall, that is significant weight. Body Mass Index is a simple way to have a general understanding on obesity, which takes into consideration the weight and the height. It's not a hundred percent perfect, but most of the time, it will suffice with regard to the needs for diagnostics measurement.

In regard to the weight, especially as related to COVID-19, there is a lot of secretion of adiponectin, a protein hormone, which is involved in regulating glucose levels as well as fatty acid breakdown. It plays a role in protecting against insulin resistance and clogging arteries and developing diabetes and cardiovascular disease. Adipokines and cytokines from the infrared abdominal fat impair the immune system response to infectious disease in general. There were significant alterations of the mechanical property of the entire respiratory system due to obesity contributing to the change in the physiology of the lung, which makes people who are overweight more susceptible to getting serious complications from COVID-19, including going on ventilators at a much higher rate.

Early on, this was still just becoming apparent. At six months into the pandemic, we had a little bit more data about obesity and Body Mass Index and how it impacts COVID-19. We noticed that although the COVID-19 morbidity rate was much higher in the older population, obesity took away the advantage of age for a lot of people, meaning younger patients were as greatly impacted as older patients if they were obese.

Later on, there was another analysis showing that a lot of the younger population who were admitted to the intensive care had some weight issue, even before they reached the obesity range, having a Body Mass Index between 28 and 30, which put them in the overweight category. These patients had three to four times greater risk of getting admitted to the ICU and having worse outcomes. Explanation was mainly about the fat cell functions, the adipose tissue, which is the extra fat in the mid part, which is called visceral adipose tissue.

Those patients with this kind of obesity, many of them have what is called insulin resistance, which is a higher level of insulin, because the body is resisting the action of the insulin. The adipose tissue, the fat tissue, recruits a lot of inflammatory factors. Some of them, it's called cytokines, and interleukin six, and tumor necrotic factor and plasminogen activating inhibitor one (PAI-1). All of this contributes to a lot of clotting issues that subsequently lead to more sickness.

Another theory involves the angiotensin converting enzyme receptors which are expressed a lot in the adipose tissue. This gave easier access for the coronavirus to enter an obese patient's body.

Another problem obese patients were dealing with was sleep apnea and other breathing issues. Many of them have limited capacity in their lungs and the diaphragm will push against the lung and lower their ability to breathe well. A larger percent of these patients needed intubation, and add to it more difficulties with intubation.

The Younger Population.

Obesity was the major factor in the younger population who became extremely sick from COVID-19. Most likely, most of the younger patients who had a lot of difficulty with COVID-19 were obese. They do have other comorbid conditions such as high blood pressure, heart disease, and even diabetes. Some of them were only obese and that was one of a major risk factor to be sick and have more complication.

A Body Mass Index of 25 is considered healthy, 25 to 30 is overweight, and more than 30 is considered obese. The ones who had their Body Mass Index over 35, they were carrying a significant amount of weight in their abdomen and that also caused a lot of pressure on the diaphragm. This made breathing much harder. This is one of the factors that contributed to the respiratory disease in COVID-19 patients who were overweight. It was harder to get enough oxygen into the lungs and into the blood due to the extra weight on the abdomen and the pressure on the diaphragm.

Another possibility why obese patient did worse is inflammation. The fat tissue itself is metabolically active and we can say that the fat tissue is the largest endocrine system because it secretes a lot of hormones and secretes a lot of inflammatory molecules. Cytokines is one of them and it is an immune protein that gets secreted in response to different kinds of sickness and it usually trigger a cascade of immune system responses in an obese patient. This cascade is much more activated and the response of the immune system in the patient who was overweight was more magnified and usually lead to more sickness.

When the tissues get overwhelmed, as discussed above, we realized that we should treat obesity seriously as it is a pre-existing condition which will increase risk for COVID-19 causing serious problems in patients. Ultimately, this takes away the advantage of young age.

Diet.

A lot of restaurants were closed, even the fast food ones. Some of them closed in the early stage of the disease. In my observation, a lot of people who were not able to go eat out and order out did gain some weight during that quarantining. However, we did see a better metabolic profile. After three months into the disease, we ordered a lot of lipid profiles and some reactive measurements such as serum reactive protein, and other factors and they were significantly better despite the change in the weight. A lot of hard working people who don't have time or

Businesses had to shut down due to COVID-19. Unfortunately for some, this close was permanent.

sometimes don't have the money to cook healthy and eat healthy used fast food for their rescue. The fast food really contributed to a much higher rate of inflammation, and unfortunately, more sickness from the disease.

Not the Norm.

Due to the widespread incidence of obesity in the United States we almost like to think this is the new norm and it's really not. A lot of physicians do not take the time to address the weight issue, especially when we have very little time to address so many issues with the pressure of the HMO and the need to produce more and all that. Again, we have to go back to what is the root of the problem. Although the patients come in for different causes, we cannot ignore the fact that they are overweight. It might seem that 60% of the patients who come to see you in adult practice are overweight, that still does not make it the norm. We still have to address it, we still have to go to the basics and talk about what is ideal body weight, not what is common, or what most people weigh.

We should not overlook this problem at all.

I thought it would be a good opportunity for a lot of my patients when they were staying home and we were doing telemedicine early in the stage of the lockdown to remind them to stay healthy and take this opportunity to work out or find a good balance in their life between exercise and eating healthy, while many of them were working from home. I always mentioned to them that when I used to see them, they would say I don't have time. I said now I'm giving you three months of time. See what you can do with it.

Many of them began walking. We saw the rate of walking go up significantly. A lot bought exercise equipment. As of September 2020, you cannot even order a treadmill as they were on backorder, as were stationary and regular bikes. The good thing was that people were picking up those habits which I'm hoping will remain as positive changes after the pandemic finally ends.

The whole pandemic experience has been a sea of blackness.

Mental Health and Coronavirus

There is no one that has not been affected by COVID-19 in some form. For many people it impacted their mental and emotional health. There has been a significant wide range of effects from coronavirus on every single person in America, if not in the world. In general, the incidence of mental health issues is quite common in America and this, if anything, had been exacerbated significantly after COVID-19 switched the world.

Statistics provided by the World Health Organization tell us that 53% of adults have been negatively impacted by COVID-19 and that number has been increasing steadily, getting worse every month.

The Forgotten Impact.

People were so busy protecting themselves against contracting the coronavirus that not a lot of attention was put on mental health, especially early on. The social isolation and the loneliness impacted mental health negatively. It is almost like a lot of patients that had anxiety became much worse and those that didn't have anxiety now know how it feels to have both rational and irrational fear about the world around them.

From the start, it appeared to not be that significant, thinking that all this would come to an end. Six months into it, we started to notice that there was no end in sight yet. Mental health abnormalities began to show up significantly at this time. A wide range of theories exist as to how and why the virus affects people. It impacted, it still impacts, everybody.

As we mentioned before, one in five people in America used to have some kind of mental health issue with drug overdosing topping the list – and this before COVID-19 stepped in to steal the stage. The suicide rate was quite high at 4.3% the year before the arrival of the coronavirus. All of this went up significantly with the pandemic, in some cases doubling or tripling or more.

Social status and the place where people were living played an important role on the impact of the coronavirus on their mental health.

From the beginning of the closing of businesses, the mandatory stay at home for non-essential workers, the prohibition of large gatherings, the requirement for quarantining following travel, and adding social (physical) distancing collectively took a large toll on those without previous issues with mental health, just as it impacted those with previously known underlying mental health issues.

Alone.

Social isolation and loneliness are both factors that impact the mental and physical health of human beings in general. Many of the people who were staying home that were not essential workers were having a lot of depression. Those that were not staying home, such as the front line workers, were exhibiting increased anxiety.

Loneliness fills the air as physical distance separates us,
as though through a fence, or maybe a wall.

After a few months in the pandemic, those in leadership roles started realizing the large toll of the virus on people beyond those that contracted the virus, especially they young adult and the elderly. For ages twelve to seventeen, anxiety and depression were generally quite common, and it doubled, at least, during this time. I spoke earlier about the isolation forced upon and felt by the elderly living in the nursing homes, which exacerbated their already present feelings of depression and dementia. For many with dementia, prior to COVID-19, it was managed well, but with the isolation, the feelings of loneliness caused these patients to act out to the point of needing greater isolation. They were pulled out of their ability to interact with others. It became a vicious cycle where the loneliness, physical distancing, and restrictions against seeing their families made their condition much worse. The mandate from those in authority to isolate them further was devastating and much worse than anyone could have ever anticipated.

Loss of Employment.

Another factor that impacted mental health issues was the loss of employment. We know that the unemployment rate went up significantly. It was almost at 14% in April of 2020. It started to get better for a bit, but with the loss of available funds for unemployment, the battle in Congress over a stimulus package, and dwindling financial security added to the mental health effects such as difficulty sleeping, eating disorders, increased alcohol consumption, and if they had access to drugs, increased drug use.

There is no near end for the employment crises, especially as we have entered into the second wave of the virus in America where we may have another lock down, further lost employment, and more isolation.

Front Line Impacts.

Healthcare workers on the front line suffered from increased mental health issues, as brought up briefly earlier. Many hospitals were overwhelmed with a large number of COVID-19 patients and the rapid increase of the demand on them and their services. Also, there was the impact of seeing a large number of deaths. None of us had experience with such a large number of fatalities in such a short period of time. Many physicians didn't have a lot of training in this, especially those trained in America. Those trained in a different part of the world may have had different experiences but nevertheless they were all unprepared for what they had seen.

Earlier in the book I presented cases of healthcare workers that committed suicide. One of them was the Emergency Room doctor from New York who previously had not suffered from mental health issues. She was unable to digest all that was happening in such a short time. This led to the unfortunate event of her suicide. Another one was the nurse who threw herself off a building following an overwhelming shift with a large number of COVID-19 admissions to the hospital.

A lot of places early on were not well prepared, especially in the cities where the virus first arrived. They were utilizing every space they could. Patients everywhere, bodies everywhere – some alive, some not. A sea of masks on patients, doctors, everyone. There was almost no human touch, except that which was medically necessary. No human expression anywhere. This took a huge toll on a lot of front line workers.

Many of these front line workers also became sick from the coronavirus, losing work and possible money. Others had to cover for those who became ill, working extra hours, beyond ideal human capacity. This increased anxiety and fatigue, which added to the fear of contracting the virus.

Getting Prepared.

A lot of front line workers, including myself, were having to write their will, just in case of the worst. I sat down with my family and I explained to them the chance that me or other healthcare providers dying was higher than for non-front line workers. I explained to them what they needed to do if I was gone. For the first time ever, we realized that there is nothing more real than death and death is closer to all of us than we ever think.

This forgotten fact about life had to be brought into the light, making it a reality. It was happening everywhere, all around us. Add to it, each one of us already knew one or two healthcare workers that had already died from or due to the coronavirus.

Necessary Changes.

We know that there will be long- and short- term impacts on mental health from this situation with COVID-19. We talk about short-term impacts such as anxiety and depression. Burn out was already high amongst healthcare workers, and with this virus spreading chaos in the hospitals, we saw this double or triple, which only brought on more anxiety to those who were sticking it out.

There was such a gap between the administration and the healthcare worker, it almost felt like the healthcare worker was the catalyst for this virus. Many healthcare workers that were not on the front line had already lost their job due to loss in hospital income from a drop in procedures and standard service income that were not being provided during the heart of the pandemic.

It almost felt like a lot of healthcare workers thought it was time for them to think about how to revise how the system worked, where so many people who were not physicians or medical personal made decisions for many hospitals and many physicians. The realization that our job is to help people, our job is to never run from responsibility, our job is to jump every time there is an opportunity to save a life or a soul. Still, the discrepancy between what we do and what the higher paid administration do made it hard to even accept the reality of the job situation, which led to greater depression, anxiety, and burn out.

A lot of physicians had looked into changing their set up at work, not necessarily their career. We thought a lot of people would be turned off from going into the medical field. While we did lose a lot of physicians, a lot of young people were choosing to enter the field. Fresh young minds thought they could save others and admission to medical school has gone up quite a bit. As an initial silver lining, the virus has increased interest in. and entrance into, the medical field.

Closures.

With the lockdown and closing of a lot of halfway houses and mental health facilities, this also impacted a lot of pre-existing mental health issues. These places provide many services, including social workers, interaction with peers, and psychological services. Due to the virus, many of these places were closed, except for acute emergency care. This made it harder for those with pre-existing anxiety and depression to get help. Luckily, a lot of physicians and psychologists offered telemedicine, which helped tremendously with keeping mental health issues in check.

Healthcare facilities and insurance companies were offering a free check-up online, sometimes with twenty-four-hour availability to help people cope. They introduced a lot of facts on how to deal with isolation and how to improve their health status while alone. For instance, ensuring that they kept their sleep schedule and took care of personal hygiene matters. A lot of people probably didn't even think about the fact that staying home and not going in to work to see anyone, increased depression and under those conditions some people were ignoring personal hygiene needs. It was also important to make sure patients ate on a regular schedule.

Recommendations.

Exercise was one of the things that helped maintain sanity. Many people took up walking because with the lockdown beginning in March, the weather started to turn nice and people wanted to be out in the good weather. For the longest time, the weather was nice, and walking afforded the opportunity to maintain distance while getting exercise in. People kept walking, as it was a good thing to change the scenery and get some fresh air, both of which are good for mental health. People were advised to do things that they enjoyed doing, not just watch television which had ugly news all day long. Lowering screen time, video game time, and social media time was important since there wasn't a lot of positivity coming from these sources.

Much like walking, horseback riding was an activity that allowed for physical distancing, fresh air, and enjoyment with extended family.

There was some advice on limiting alcohol and drugs. Since not in the office and around others, some were drinking a bit more. This was something people wanted to do. The drinking was due to social isolation and boredom. We wanted to remind people to keep the number of drinks down, because drinking a lot of alcohol would impact the immune system and create greater risk for infection. Also, we were serious about not exceeding the limits on alcohol intake as it would cause such an inhibition in making sure you are still protected and you are properly using personal protective equipment and avoiding contact with any source of the infection. Basically, cover up and avoid unnecessary in-person communication with others.

College Interrupted.

Anxiety is quite common for college students in general. After the pandemic arrived, most of the colleges were not holding classes in person. And when they did hold classes that needed to meet in person, it became chaotic and stressful over who was following rules or not, who wore their mask and maintained physical distancing. Everyone was watching everyone, playing the policing game and the blame game. They were trying to force the rules or judge others who were not following the rules. This caused such chaos for the college student life. They couldn't just go on in life. It was interrupted by COVID-19 which brought them back from spring break to unchartered territories This was one added layer of learning in a time of higher-than-average anxiety.

Even in the fall, schools remained closed to in-person classes. They could not work with other students or have in-person human contact, which is actually needed for humans. What is worse for these young people is the uncertainty. There is still no end in sight. Most colleges are planning to maintain virtual learning of some kind through the Spring of 2021. And who knows what will happen beyond that.

High school seniors are having the worst interruption on their life. They were hopeful for an amazing year as they prepared to transition out of their childhood into adulthood. They wanted to do college visits and trying to get a scholarship. Athletes especially worked so hard up until this point to get scholarships and it isn't possible now with sports having been cancelled for the time being. There were a lot of missed opportunities for many students who will not be able to afford attending the college of their choice due to less scholarships available to students. Imagine some of the students doing a sport for their entire life and now nothing. With no sporting events for a long time, this has pulled the ground out from under young people whose entire identity centered around their sports life. They lost themselves and their will to even try. This along with not being able to be with their friends and just be a young person enjoying this time in life that is all about transitioning into adulthood at one's own pace. Now, the only interaction is on social media or some other online venue. While connecting with friends online was good, it was weighted down with distracting negative messaging that defeats the purpose of these students seeking connections with their friends on social media. It was hard for a lot of people to go to social media for support.

More recommendations.

The World Health Organization (WHO) has a message for the general population about referring to those patients suffering from COVID-19. First, they ask that we be empathetic towards those that affected, who are from all countries. Don't refer to people as COVID-19 cases or diseased. They are people who have COVID-19 or are being treated for the coronavirus. We are advised to focus on the patient not the illness, so not a COVID-19 patient, but a patient who contracted the virus. It is important that the focus is on the person that would be missed by loved ones if they left this world.

With this, the WHO emphasized minimizing exposure to excess news, especially negative stories, about the coronavirus. And most important here, find a trusted source for news about the virus and its impact on society. They further go on recommending that you be protected and protect others, assisting others without letting your guard down. Find opportunities to find positivity in your life and passing it on to others. For instance, some people found satisfaction in helping healthcare workers in some way, whether it was buying a meal or creating more masks. I know from my corner of the world, local restaurants were sending food nonstop to the hospital almost every day for several months. If you want to send food to the hospital now, you have to be added to a long list and wait your turn to serve.

For the healthcare worker feeling pressure that left them needing to talk to someone, there are resources provided by organizations such as the American Medical Associates (AMA) and the World Health Organization (WHO). They provide guidance on how to cope with stress and deal with family. Many people were not even staying at home during the first weeks of the pandemic. We were not 100% sure about the transmission and many colleagues were not going home. They had little ones at home and were afraid of exposing them.

With time, we learned better how to make sure to leave the clothes we wore at work at work and then shower before interacting with any family members. It also caused such a stigma and fear. I remember crossing the street to talk to elderly neighbors in our new community. I wanted to introduce myself and let them know I was a physician and if they needed anything to just ask. Due to COVID-19, however, I was undesirable to talk to, to interact with. People feared the exposure healthcare workers clearly brought with them – they must carry the virus with them everywhere.

Stay Connected.

Healthcare workers were encouraged to talk to their supervisors and colleagues if feeling anxiety or burn out. Keeping those lines of communication open was important to ensure mental health issues didn't overwhelm them. This advice isn't just for the healthcare worker though. We advised this to the elderly who were among those who faced the greatest risk from the virus. They needed to not be around people, yet they still needed to connect with people. This is where technology played a helpful role, allowing some to keep in touch without the risk, even if at the loss of human touch.

For those who live alone, this is especially important. Reaching out to family and friends helps them to stay grounded in the positive. Those with family were advised to embrace them and enjoy the forced time for closeness.

Happy birthday masked dance in the garage with family.

Family and Coronavirus

———◆———

Throughout history, during times of sorrow, the people that individuals rely on most are those around them – usually family. During the time of the pandemic, people were rooted in their homes and consistently around their family. They went from busy work schedules and the hustle of everyday life to the familiar. As the news of the coronavirus became a more substantial part in all of our lives, the idea of being secluded in our homes caused worry but a sense of relief simultaneously.

As the cases began to rise, individuals of all ages began to face the idea of death. The idea of our own mortality isn't something we usually face. From doing daily tasks to doing something as simple as brushing our teeth, we as humans are made to be distracted from death until we are forced to face it. During the virus, however, everyone in the world was surrounded by the idea of death. In times like this, we can't help but apply devastating situations to our own lives. More and more people began to write wills, as the television reported news of no room for the dead bodies.

My Family.

Personally, I experienced this fear with my family when the pandemic first began. My mother, one of the strongest women I know, was crippled by fear as all her children worked tirelessly on the front lines facing the sickness face-to-face, because five of the seven children are medical doctors and two of the seven are dentists. While the pandemic occupied everyone's minds, the stress of this disease was was extremely high for my family since so many of us are part of the medical field.

This pandemic has affected individuals of all ages. It has impacted all aspects of life, from the news, to our daily lives, people of all generations have had their lives uprooted by this pandemic. As the next generation is forced to be confined to their home, my twelve-year-old nephew is beginning to consider the life of lockdown as life's new norm.

The next generation is habituating to new terms like social distancing, as it is the young who are too much into their digital world and now add to it that they can survive doing everything without interacting personally with any one including eLearning. We have been worried that we were creating an aloof generation by making the digital world available to them from every angle, and this fear has heightened. If they decide not to go to school or college and instead do it all online, can we stop them?

Maybe not.

Daughter and I.

Disaster brings people together.

This statement can't be more accurate to anyone than me. When I lost my husband, she lost her beloved father who dedicated his whole life to her, literally, he did. He quit his job and stayed home to take care of her and take her to the hockey world, which is consuming. They became best buddies, they were inseparable. Meanwhile, I was enjoying what America was offering me: success, warmth of my patients. I think they were enjoying the warmth of a Middle Eastern doctor.

I was fulfilled, my daughter and my husband were happy.

That didn't last long, at age nine, she lost her whole world when her father passed away suddenly in her presence. I came back from the funeral to realize I didn't know this child, I needed to know her. We became close, we traveled the world and I realized how this person who up to now was a stranger to me, is almost a copy of me plus the athletic part from her dad. I was so happy to be in her company, we almost were not separable.

We visited most of Europe, we went as far as Russia and we went a few times to Alaska, a few times to the Middle East. We learned a lot in our travels. We made a lot of friends along the way, we wrote our journal together, we dressed up every night. We went out for fancy dinners. We became close, a mother's dream came true.

This closeness did not last long. High school came and we were strangers again.

Then, the pandemic came. I picked her up from school in mid-March and little did I know, we became buddies again. At the start we were doing our own stuff, then we started baking together and cooking together and at night we had our routine, playing ping pong ball and watching a few of our favorites shows, after which we had our special snacks where each one of us would surprise the other with food from our past or from a vacation place we have been to.

A month or two into the pandemic, we started getting sick of the plain white mask, we started making fancy masks with figures, birds, flowers, lips, butterflies, etc. She started selling them, she figured out she would not be able to get a summer job with the widespread layoffs and that was her way of making money and having fun and spending time with her mother.

We were making masks for my daughter to sell and she made this one so my patients could see my lips when I talked.

The business took off and she started her website, moodmask.net. She started making Halloween masks and Christmas ones too. She also made me the clear bottom mask, she said to see patients smile and read their expressions, but deep inside she did it for me not to get frustrated when my hard of hearing patients can't understand my accent under the covered mask.

We used to celebrate her birthday every year in a series of parties, but this year was a garage party with a dance wearing masks. It was a grand time.

It has been a really pleasant experience to be home with the family for an extended period of time. We started visiting outside, then came inside where every family took one corner to keep six feet apart from each family.

The Kids' View.

The kids in the family had a different views. Some did different things from thinking the virus was the devil coming to get us. Others were just annoyed by the interruption of their social life. My nephew saw some advantage to it as seen in his essay.

Extended Family.

The distant family who were not in the medical field were scared to get in touch with us at first but then they began doing it with caution. We started new routines with my sisters and my mom, walking for a few miles every day. We were outside, not too close to each other and that was a great start to a good habit. We are hoping to continue that with or without coronavirus.

A major event in my life was when Coronavirus started. I began to look at the world from a new perspective. I stopped taking things for granted. The outbreak made me respect technology. However, it also showed me just how much trust we put in it. I used to think of social time as a thing I'll always have. However, these hard times have disconnected me from the world. Luckily, I was able to quarantine with my next-door neighbor, so I at least have someone that isn't my parents. We connected while we disconnected from everyone else. Once things started opening I felt relieved. For example, when tennis opened back up with certain regulations I was still happy. Even though we can't touch the balls, or get close, I still had fun. If it hadn't been for that amount of time without anyone near me I would have been angry about these regulations.

Technology these days is great. We can still go to school without fear of spreading coronavirus. I do all of my tests, quizzes, and practices online. I am able to see and hear my entire class, including the teacher. I can learn almost as well. Many people are waiting for school to open back up, with me included, but it isn't that bad to be online. I feel that it was the right decision to keep my school online. It may make my learning a little bit worse, but we are contributing to the community to stop the virus and save lives.

Technology doesn't always work. For example, earlier today my wifi crashed for about forty-five minutes and I was unable to do anything school-related during school because of that. Luckily I was able to do some of that at my friend's house, which still had wifi. If that had been at regular school, I would have been unaffected and could have continued my learning with the rest of the class. We put too much trust in technology, so when there is a glitch, there are serious consequences.

In conclusion, the coronavirus outbreak was a major event in my life. It made me really grateful for an interactive community. It made me feel the greatness of technology. And it made me see that we put too much trust in technology. As many people say, you don't know how important something really is until you lose it.

A story from my young eleven-year-old nephew, unedited.

Pets and Animals.

The pets were the one who had been surprised the most. Owners were
not leaving. Pets got to have their owners around most of the day. They
became more attached to their owners, including my own cat who sits on
my shoulder while I do telemedicine. Or on my lap while I am writing.
Or by my feet when I am sleeping.

We started bird watching, we had time during the day to see birds, it was amazing what happened to nature when we were busy at work. It has been so much fun to watch the birds outside the kitchen windows.

The switched world has created new products, like this mask hanger.

Life After Coronavirus

———◆———

Life will be forever changed.

Nothing will be the same.

Again.

September 11 changed life in America. I remember vividly how life changed 180 degrees for me, and maybe a little bit less for others, but we noticed significant changes in life in America. We noticed significant change in the way people are thinking, how they accept others, and of course, everything had changed in regard to the securities at airports, for air travel.

The new rules came after that process for more protection and at the same time, people were much more welcoming to foreigners and diversity before September 11. People were curious. They had a beautiful, steady, boring, luxurious American life and it was an entertainment to meet another culture and other people and get to know their food, their life, the way they act, and that did not continue after September 11.

These foreigners, anybody who did not look like the "regular" American; they are scary. They're not an interest anymore. They are a threat. We knew that and we knew life would never be the same in America. After the pandemic, life will not be the same. Not just in America, but in the whole world. A lot of things will change. A lot of things have changed with COVID-19 during the year 2020.

A New Future.

There is no going back.

When the changes are made, we start noticing already and we will see way more on a much bigger scale, that eliminating office space could be positive or negative. A lot of jobs can be done from a small space at home with a computer. This created both advantage and disadvantage. A lot of jobs will be gone. Obviously, the fact was that companies were forced to have employees complete their work from home, or they were forced to lay off a lot of people. This showed that the work was doable in a new landscape or was simply not needed at all. Ultimately, this meant eliminate the workspace and at times the job. A lot of factors played a role and we have yet see the outcome fully be realized in the workforce.

For instance, in the food service industry consumer needs have shifted. I will choose not to go to a crowded restaurant again. A lot of restaurants were overpacking customers and I always talked about the greed of America. Businesses are about making money, yes, but the busier they are and the more money they want to make, the less they care about the customer. In the interest of making greater profit, a good busy restaurant will strive to be busier and they put the chairs closer to each other. You can barely hear yourself talking. You can always hear the neighbors' conversation.

Another thing potentially eliminated, the crowded airline with no room for people. You probably noticed the seats were getting smaller and smaller to pack more people into the plane with no room to move around. They were making huge profits, providing evidence that there is no limit for greed and how much more money they want to make. It just gets to be too much. Hopefully, the societal changes caused by COVID-19 will scale down this practice of a crowded flight.

Telemedicine.

Also, interesting to see the growth of another aspect of the healthcare sector. Telemedicine took over a lot of healthcare and part of it has some advantage. Even if you are living so far in a remote area, and you need access to medical care, you might be able to get access to all kinds of specialists all over the world not available to them otherwise. Plus, a lot of people may not be able to drive themselves and or can't get access to public transportation system, which was not advised anyway during the time of the coronavirus.

I'm not a big fan of telemedicine but it serves some purposes. The problem, actually being a presentable doctor and having social skills and having a good bedside manner probably won't matter much anymore. The whole healthcare system will forever change. Of course, there will still be a lot of manual in-person work that simply cannot be done via telemedicine. For instance, shots, placing devices, diabetes specific technology of Continuous Glucose Monitoring System (CGMS) to measure blood sugar levels day and night. This is a great tool to see how the stress of the virus, family situations, and financial conditions, affect the blood sugar, all of which is hard to do without being in the office.

With telemedicine we will lose all in-person human contact discussed previously.

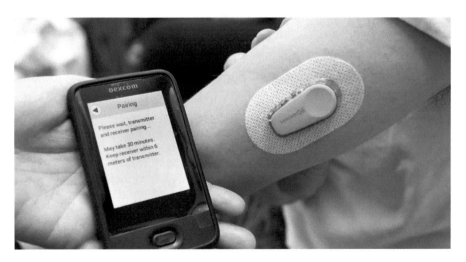

The Continuous Glucose Monitoring System is an essential piece of equipment for some diabetes patients. Unfortunately, with telemedicine, placing this would not be possible.

Pharma.

Obviously, we don't need all these fancy drug representatives created by corporations who get paid quite well. They dress up. They go to the doctors' offices and they present their data, and they get to serve their product. We did not have a direct drug company representative for three months between March until July. In July, a few drug companies began sending reps out, but a lot of the servicing was done virtually.

Obviously, we survived.

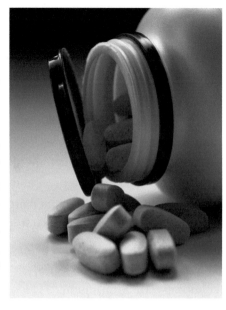

Prescriptions are a huge part of the healthcare system in America, even during the pandemic.

We served our patients, and we knew what a good product for them was and wasn't. We all have a lot of access to a lot of data, however, in some parts of the country having a direct representative for education and for access to medicine will be huge. I would say probably 20% of our patients count on samples to get them started at least and then not to waste their money by buying products that may or may not work for them. Sampling is a huge part of our practices. Even with that, looking at how the pharmaceutical company will be shaped up after COVID-19, I think it will forever change significantly.

Maybe they don't need to spend a lot of money on marketing, maybe they can lower the price a little bit. Maybe they will have those drug reps work on the different things, maybe doing some health project or some statistics or some data collection to even improve our medical system and transferring it from sick care to healthcare for real.

Fast Food.

Fast food, that's the real enemy of America.

We have to look first at the positive of fast food. It was a way to feed busy people at low prices, but some of the food came as poor quality designed for keeping the price low. The fact that it was not available for a while and people were able to survive, maybe that will help lower their use of fast food. Maybe that will help make their life healthier and make them better able to fight disease. We knew that the disease hit the low socio-economic neighborhoods and many of them count on fast food as a source of feeding in general. We knew that wasn't good for them. We knew that the cost of obesity, and one of the causes is the easy access and the price of fast food. That was another factor which made people sicker from COVID-19.

Money.

The sudden loss of income and job and pandemic made a lot of people think about their finances. I've been shocked how many people did not have even a reserve in their bank account to survive for a week or two. I think people will think twice about their finances after the pandemic is over, hopefully, for a better preparation for another disaster.

A good rule of thumb is to have enough money in savings to cover six months of living expenses, left untouched. Needless to say, 90% of the working forces didn't have that which is a sad fact in the wealthiest country – America. Americans have had to wait on Congress to stop their political fight to provide for the people. Here is a time we can take a lesson from other countries which took the steps to provide for their people. I hope that the leaders will step up and provide to Americans a decent living regardless of the pandemic or political gain.

My daughter and husband baking bread, together.

The Silver Lining

———◆———

Every cloud has its silver lining. And we did have some silver lining in the cloud of COVID-19 as the catalyst for change, bringing up some positivity to the post-COVID-19 world. However, we know that the world would forever be different after COVID-19. That's why I thought this book about the switch from before to after the coronavirus was needed to bring the point of significant changes due to COVID-19.

The workforce would be forever changed. Yes, we lost a lot of jobs. The unemployment rate at some point was 10%. Of course, we expect it to go back to pre-coronavirus. At the same time, obviously a lot of jobs could have been eliminated or are now being done from home and that will never switch back. We will lose a lot of jobs, but also new ones may be added. The world will be different, evolving, as it always has done. We just have to keep an open mind.

Job.

A lot of people were furloughed, and thanks to unemployment benefits, they were getting paid to not work. Many of them realize this is a golden opportunity, there will never be another time in their life where they will have such an opportunity where money is coming in and they're not asked to demand any of their time. No more excuse for not having time to do things like getting healthy or getting the job of your dreams. The coronavirus gave us time – lots of time. We have time when we are home, we can think about what that dream job is that we've always wanted.

Now, meet Tanya. Tanya was working in a factory and raising her kids. One of her kids is in college and the other just finished college. She kept thinking, one day, when the kids are all grown. Well the kids are all grown now and the one day did not come until it was forced upon her. Now that day is here. The factory closed due to fear of contamination and a crowded environment. Tanya was sent home and she was still getting paid. There was no known return day, with three months, at least, to think about what she wanted to do when one day came.

A key to healthy food is homemade. A new trend in restaurants is to market their food as "homemade," where they will only have clean ingredients going into it, no preservatives, everything will be made fresh. Tanya thought about selling the fresh foods that she liked to cook. She started practicing on her family. I remember her sitting in the kitchen trying different recipes for corn biscuit cake and pies. Everybody enjoyed her cooking and then she began passing it on to the neighbors and the neighbors began asking her if she could make it for them for a price.

She started that and then, with the help of her college kids, she was able to put up a website. She did not have the capital to begin a big business, so she began small. She would take an order and deliver it within 48 hours, so she would only have to buy a few ingredients at a time. By month three, she was so busy, and everybody was telling everybody about her. She started getting somebody to help her in the house. At that time there were a lot of people who lost their jobs and they were happy to help a little bit, doing stuff and building her dream.

Needless to say, Tonya decided not to ever go back to her factory work and she's happy. She keeps saying thank you COVID-19, although it's cheesy to say. If it wasn't for this lockdown, she would have never had the opportunity to do it.

Relationships.

There we were, people home with whoever they decide to spend the rest of their life with. Together we had nothing to do, especially for the first few weeks of the lockdown except being with each other. Thank goodness for Netflix. There is no more doing, there's only being and unfortunately a lot of relationship effort was consumed by actions, such as going places, participating in activities, hanging with friends. Constantly. This is all gone, and now the focus is on the relationship effort.

To build on our relationships, we did things together. For instance, we made masks together so my daughter could sell them.

What you see is what you get, even if that is not what you want. A lot of people recalculated their relationships and realized that we are young and healthy right now. When we are older, we will not be going out that often. We will not be having a lot of doing. This is what we will have. Is this what we want? That's why we saw significant change in the divorce rate. The filing rate for divorce was the highest at any time of the American life.

Domestic violence call-in lines and homes for battered women were open and reaching capacity. These times so close to the abuser became a huge reality check for society. We have started to recognize the importance of paying attention to the needs of our neighbors, even as we maintain a physically masked distance. This is a time when people need a good companion and somebody who will bring peace and support to each others' lives. This is how we protect the vulnerable and maintain the American dream.

All this checked long list had been playing in a lot of people's minds and it was the appropriate time to do it. A lot of relationships ended. Unfortunately, there were not a lot of opportunities for opening new relationships. All this was a bit on hold for a while although social media was the rescue for a lot of loneliness at this time in a lot of people's lives.

Friendship.

Doing something, showing some appreciation went a long way. Going back to the friendships, it was a great time to clear up your list of friends. The only ones you thought about talking to or calling, those are your true friends and those are the ones you want to keep. Keep them on your side, for rainy days and for sunny days.

Many of us have gone through a lot of friendships during our life and some realize maybe sooner rather than later that negative relationship will bring nothing except negativity to your life. It took a while until they were able to get rid of this but during the COVID-19 time you really did not keep in touch with your negative people, especially with all the negativity going around and all the dark environment. You needed somebody who would bring you up, not bring you down. You need somebody whose positive energy would be contagious.

The physical distancing took its toll, as we were regulated behind computers. At least this allowed us some connection and time to rebalance our electronic presence.

It was a great time to clean up your list of friends. However, that did not mean that you don't support the one who needed support. I thought that COVID-19 brought out the best of people and the worst of people. It was so important to see how people were acting, especially with selfishness and greediness getting worse. At the same time, the givers of the world had a beautiful opportunity to assist others with joy and excitement, because that is what kindness is all about. A kind word and the kind act went a long, long way. It's almost like people were hungry for kindness. They were hungry for soft words, especially when you are eliminating the smile factor. It's amazing how expression and smile helps connect the whole world together and now we lost that part of connectivity.

Education.

Obviously, we survived school online. A lot of colleges were having a lot of limitations on how many students they could admit due to space limitation of personnel who could teach them, oversee them. Recently, instead of having 200 people in the class, you're able to have at least 300 or 400 online. That had been great for a lot of students who were on waitlist for a lot of colleges.

All of a sudden, the colleges can absorb more students online and many of them would have never dreamt of being in this college or

Community members rally around teachers and staff to show support for the extra work from teaching virtually.

that college and sure they get admitted there. Another possibility is that a lot of students have anxiety regarding social events, and interacting with people. The eLearning, although it has advantages and disadvantages, was great for many students, and there were a lot of stories in the news about somebody who excelled on online learning, especially the one with attention deficit and some kind of social anxiety disorders. This is one of the advantages of the post pandemic.

Of course, it isn't all good. For teachers, it takes much more time to teach online, sometimes as much as double or triple the time for each student. Then there are the connection issues. At least, the virtual education landscape allows for a different way to see the world and continued interpersonal contact, even if not the same as face-to-face.

Traffic and Pollution.

Hasn't traffic been wonderful?

Pollution has gone down significantly. Earlier in this stage of the pandemic, when there was no traffic at all, in so many big cities, many cities were able to see clearly. they were able to breathe much better in California, in China, and in some other crowded countries. The pollution is less now, although theoretically we are open again, and we are back to practice, back to doing business, of course not like before. Many of those jobs had been switched to online. Students online. So much online.

This has made a huge advantage to the traffic number one, to the pollution number two. It was never an issue during the pandemic to drive anytime of the day. As a physician when I had an emergency before COVID-19, I would cringe when I was supposed to go back to the hospital around rush hour. The rush hour definition has changed significantly after the pandemic.

Creativity.

In the time of the pandemic, a lot of people have sought out their creative sides. I asked a lot of my

The roads were near empty during the pandemic, filled mostly with essential workers off to do their duty.

friends, "Didn't you always want to have the time to do this or that but you couldn't? Didn't you always want to be creative and have time to do stuff?"

Well, the time is now. Take for example Danielle. She wanted to open a baking business. The pandemic and her lost job gave her that ability. Sonia started her own Greeting Cards Company.

Gardening was on the rise during the uncertainty of the pandemic.
Fresh vegetables were on a lot more plates than usual.

Many people wanted to do home projects and that's another advantage. A lot of handymen or construction businesses have been busy because people really wanted to work on their home when they are home and those big fixing projects have been up significantly.

A lot of people have started doing gardening and growing their own vegetables. That was message from our previous First Lady about home gardening and growing your own vegetables. One of the things I noticed was a "salad bowl" has been sold so fast in so many stores. What is a "salad bowl," you ask. It's a plant growing lettuce, chives, arugula, different kinds of greens. You will grow it at home and just keep watering it and cut it and use it to make your homemade salad. Instead of buying the green and not using them and they go bad and there's nothing like your own homemade and homegrown salad.

A lot of people grew their own vegetables.

When the pandemic started in March, it was just the time to start planting either flowers or vegetables and sure enough by the end of August, a lot of fruit from their work had paid off. Even in our own house, we've been eating home grown tomatoes and cucumbers with all the greenery from mint to parsley to lettuce and arugula from our own garden.

Whoever was in a mood for taking lessons could obviously do that. Many websites existed before and popped up during to learn just about anything you want. I'll give you an example about myself. I always want to be a drummer, and there's no way I would have those lessons before the pandemic. During, I needed something to let off the pressure of COVID-19 practice, changes, politics. Drumming was one of my outlets thanks to the online lessons. When I logged in to look at and take lessons, there were a few hundred different kinds. You can do any lessons you want, learn anything now that we have more time.

Exercise.

The gym closed and a lot of people thought that gym was the only place to exercise. However, they learned fast enough that you can exercise anywhere, even in a jail cell. Walking and biking rose significantly. A lot of people turned a corner of their house to a gym. Another thing that has been noticed is that gym equipment are nowhere to be found anymore, as noted earlier. But again, people learn to be creative and then they don't have the excuse that I don't have time to go to the gym. If you have five to ten minutes, you can go to the gym, the gym in your house. There's so many YouTube videos, you can just log on to any of them. They are free and they are wonderful.

A lot of people can utilize the videos, and I usually advise my patients to do so, because a closed gym does not mean no exercise. There is no excuse when you can use YouTube videos for healthier living.

With exercising at home and walking and even eating healthier, although people did gain weight and I joked around, they call it COVID-19 because the average weight gain was 19 pounds. Although, of course, that's not why they called the COVID-19. But we saw a significant improvement in metabolic profile, a lot of people had their cholesterol improved. Their blood sugar improved, despite them, probably eating more but they're eating healthier food again like the number one enemy to all doctors in America.

Fast food pick up, take out, and eating at restaurants had gone down significantly and that's reflected well in a lot of patients. We saw this by June when we began doing blood tests that showed great metabolic improvement. In just a few months, we readjusted our lifestyles with healthier food and exercise which creates healthier people. I hope this change in healthy lifestyles continues with people decreasing their weight and improving their eating habits, thus improving overall health habits and the immune system, which is the most important weapon to fight this coronavirus.

Reading was one of the few activities that increased significantly. Thank goodness for the library or the online access. We have a great library system, and they were available for curbside pickup and drop off.

Before or after the switch, humans are resilient beautiful beings.

Conclusion

———◆———

It's been chaos in every way imagined. The rules were not clear. Americans make up 5% of the world's population and have 20% of the world's morbidy from COVID-19. This is a noticeable disparity.

Something went wrong with regard to this whole pandemic. Let us not play the blame game. Instead, we should look back and learn from our experiences. We can do better in future waves of this illness or another disaster that we have yet to see unfold. We may contract this virus and most likely most of us will be okay. That cannot be said for the elderly and the unfortunate of us with underlying diseases. A little inconvenience may go a long way to protect everyone.

Let us do it right for them. Let us do it right for all of us.

Imagine people who have to deal with their medical condition most of their life, from patients with diabetes who have to check their sugar levels constantly, thinking about their disease every time they want to eat, to the one with heart or lung diseases, for whom taking a breath or a step is a chore for them. And yet some people are complaining about the "chore" of wearing a mask.

Think about how much we need each other. Just like the human body, if one part is not good, the rest of the body will suffer. That is how society functions. If we all don't do the right thing, we will not survive.

It sometimes takes a disaster to bring the best out in people, in societies. Let us use this pandemic as a turning point to bring out the best version of us. Together we can think of a better way to ensure humanity moves forward, in America, in the world. We can especially count on the scientists and the healthcare professionals, true heroes in my mind, to lay the groundwork.

And maybe, we can *switch* back to some of what we knew before.

References

———◆———

1. American Association of Clinical Endocrinology (AACE). Website and other communication. 2020. https://www.aace.com/

2. American Diabetes Association (ADA). Website and other communication. 2020. https://www.diabetes.org/

3. Ayanian JZ. Tallying the toll of excess deaths from COVID-19. JAMA Health Forum. 2020:1(7):e200832 DOI:10.1001/jamahealthforum.2020.0832

4. Aytogan H, Ayintap E, Ozkalay Yilmaz N. Detection of coronavirus disease 2019 viral material on environmental surfaces of an ophthalmology examination room. JAMA Ophthalmol. Published Online 3 August 2020. DOI:10.1001/jamaophthalmol. 2020.3154

5. Barbieri JS, Frieden IJ, Nagler AR. Isotretinoin, patient saety, and patient-centered care: time to reform iPledge. JAMA Dermatol. 2020:156(1):21-22. DOI:10.1001/jamadermatol.2019.3270

6. Barnett ML, Grabowski DC. Nursing homes are "ground zero" for COVID-19 pandemic. JAMA Health Forum. 2020:1(3):e200369. DOI:10.1001/jamahealthforum.2020.0369

7. Bikdeli B, Madhavan MV, Jimenez D, et al; Global COVID-19 Thrombosis Collaborative Group, Endorsed by the ISTH, NATF, ESVM, and the IUA, Supported by the ESC Working Group on Pulmonary Circulation and Right Ventricular Function. COVID-19 and thrombotic or thromboembolic disease: implications for prevention, antithrombotic therapy, and follow-up. J Am Coll Cardiol. 2020:75(23):2950-2973. DOI:10.1016/j.jacc.2020.04.031

8. Bommakanti NIK, Zhou Y, Ehrlich JR, et al; SOURCE Consortium. Application of the sight outcomes research collaborative ophthalmology data repository for triaging patients with glaucoma and clinic appointments during pandemics such as COVID-19. JAMA Ophthalmol. Published Online 17 July 2020. DOI:10.1001/jamaophthalmol.2020.2974

9. Boyarsky BJ, Werbel WA, Durand CM, et al. Early national and center-level changes to kidney transplantation in the United States during the COVID-19 epidemic. Am J Transplant. Published Online 28 June 2020. DOI:10.1111/ajt.16167

10. Buntin MB, Gavulic KA. Safely reopening schools—learning amid a pandemic. JAMA Health Forum. 2020:1(8):e201054. DOI:10.1001/jamahealthforum.2020.1054

11. Cavallo II, Donoho DA, Forman HP. Hospital capacity and operations in the coronavirus disease 2019 (COVID-19) pandemic—planning for the Nth patient. JAMA Health Forum. 2020:1(3):e200345. DOI:10.1001/jamahealthforum.2020.0345

12. Center for Disease Control and Prevention (CDC). Website and other communication. 2020. https://www.cdc.gov/

13. Center for Disease Control and Prevention (CDC). NHANES response rates and population totals. Published Online 4 August 2020. https://wwwn.cdc.govinchs/nhanes/ResponseRates.aspx

14. Center for Disease Control and Prevention (CDC). An investigation of nonresponse bias and sample characteristics in the 2017-2018 National Health and Nutrition Examination Survey. CDC National Center for Health Statistics. 2020.https://www.cdc.gov/nchs/data/nhanes/analyticguidelines/17-18-sampling-variability-nonresponse-508.pdf

15. Chan L, Chaudhary K, Saha A, et al. Acute kidney injury in hospitalized patients with COVID-19. medRxiv. Print 8 May 2020. DOI:101101/2020.05.04.20090944

16. Deng Y, Liu W, Liu K, et al. Clinical characteristics of fatal and recovered cases of coronavirus disease 2019 (COVID-19) in Wuhan, China. Chin Med J (Engl). 2020:133(11):1261-1267. DOI:10.1097/CM9.0000000000000824

17. Dorfman D, Raz M. Mask exemptions during the COVID-19 pandemic—a new frontier for clinicians. JAMA Health Forum. 2020:1(7):e200810. DOI:10.1001/jamahealthforum.2020.0810

18. Droesch C, Hoang M, DeSancho M, Lee E-J, Magro C, Harp J. Livedoid and purpuric skin eruptions associated with coagulopathy in severe COVID-19. JAMA Dermatol. Pubished Online 5 August 2020. DOI:10.1001/jamadermatol.2020.2800

19. Essien UR, Venkataramani A. Data and policy solutions to address racial and ethnic disparities in the COVID-19 pandemic. JAMA Health Forum. 2020:1(4):e200535. DOI:10.1001/jamahealthforum.2020.0535

20. Felfeli T, Mandelcorn ED. Assessment of simulated respiratory droplet spread during an ophthalmologic slitlamp examination. JAMA Ophthalmol. Published Online 18 August 2020. DOI:10.1001/jamaophthalmol.2020.3472

21. Fosbol EL, Butt JH, Ostergaard L, et al. Association of angiotensin-converting enzyme inhibitor or angiotensin receptor blocker use with COVID-19 diagnosis and mortality. JAMA. 2020:324(2):168-177. DOI:10.1001/jama.2020.11301

22. Galvan Casas C, Catala A, Carretero Hernandez G, et al. Classification of the cutaneous manifestations of COVID-19: a rapid prospective nationwide consensus study in Spain with 375 cases. Br J Dermatol 2020 183(1):71-77 10.1111/bjd.19163

23. Gluckman TJ, Wilson MA, Chiu ST, et al. Case rates, treatment approaches, and outcomes in acute myocardial infarction during the coronavirus disease 2019 pandemic. JAMA Cordial. Published Online 7 August 2020. DOI:10.1001/jamacardio.2020. 3629

24. Goldfarb DS, Benstein JA, Zhdanova O, et al. Impending shortages of kidney replacement therapy for COVID-19 patients. Clin J Am Soc Nephrol. 2020:15(6):880-882. DOI:10.2215/0N,05180420

25. Gostin LO. The great coronavirus pandemic of 2019-7 critical lessons. JAMA Health Forum. 2020:1(8):e201043. DOI:10.1001/jamahealthforum.2020.1043

26. Grummer-Strawn LM, Reinold C, Krebs NF; Centers for Disease Control and Prevention (CDC). Use of World Health Organization and CDC growth charts for children aged 0-59 months in the United States. MMWR Recomm Rep. 2010:59(RR-9):1-15.

27. Guan WJ, Ni ZY, Hu Y, et al. Clinical characteristics of coronavirus disease 2019 in China. N Engl J Med. 2020:382(18):1708-1720. DOI:10.1056/NEJMoa2002032

28. Inciardi RM. Lupi L, Zaccone G, et al. Cardiac involvement in a patient with coronavirus disease 2019 (COVID-19). JAMA Cordial. 2020:5(7):819-824. DOI:10.1001/jamacardio.2020.1096

29. Ingram DD, Malec DJ, Makuc DM, et al. National Center for Health Statistics guidelines for analysis of trends. Vital Health Stat 2. 2018:2(179)1-71.

30. Jun ISY, Hui KKO, Songbo PZ. Perspectives on coronavirus disease 2019 control measures for ophthalmology clinics based on a Singapore center experience. JAMA Ophthalmol. 2020:138(5):435-436. DOI:10.1001/jamaophthalmo1.2020.1288

31. Kansagra AP, Goyal MS, Hamilton S, Albers GW. Collateral effect of COVID-19 on stroke evaluation in the United States. N Engl J Med. 2020:383(4):400-401. DOI:10.1056/NEJMc2014816

32. Kelly AS, Barlow SE, Rao G, et al; American Heart Association Atherosclerosis. Hypertension and Obesity in the Young Committee of the Council on Cardiovascular Disease in the Young. Council on Nutrition, Physical Activity and Metabolism, and Council on C Severe obesity in children and adolescents: identification, associated health risks, and treatment approaches: a scientific statement from the American Heart Association. Circulation. 2013:128(15):1689-1712. DOI:10.1161/CIR.0b013e3182a5cfb3

33. Kliger AS, Silberzweig J. Mitigating risk of COVID-19 in dialysis facilities. Clin J Am Soc Nephrol. 2020:15(5):707-709. DOI:10.2215/CJN.03340320

34. Lai PH, Lancet EA, Weiden MD, et al. Characteristics associated with out-of-hospital cardiac arrests and resuscitations during the novel coronavirus disease 2019 pandemic in New York City. JAMA Cordial. Published Online 19 June 2020. DOI:10.1001/jamacardio.2020.2488

35. Lester JC, Lia JL, Zhang L, Okoye GA, Linos E. Absence of images of skin of colour in publications of COVID-19 skin manifestations. Br J Derm. Published Online 29 May 2020. DOI:10.1111/bjd.19258

36. Lindner D, Fitzek A, Brauninger H, et al. Cardiac infection with SARS-CoV-2 in confirmed COVID-19 autopsy cases. JAMA Cordial. Published Online 27 July 2020. DOI:10.1001/jamacardio.2020.3551

37. Louapre C, Collongues N, Stankoff B, et al; Covisep Investigators. Clinical charactertistics and outcomes in patients with coronavirus disease 2019 and multiple sclerosis. JAMA Neurol. Published Online 26 June 2020. DOI:10.1001/jamaneurol.2020.2581

38. Loupy A, Aubert O, Reese PP, et al. Organ procurement and transplantation during the COVID-19 pandemic. Lancet. 2020:395(10237):e95-e96. DOI:101016/50140-6736(20)31040-0

39. Madigan LM, Micheletti RG, Shinkai K How dermatologists can learn and contribute at the leading edge of the COVID-19 global pandemic. JAMA Dermatol. 2020:156(7):733-734. DOI:10.1001/jamadermato1.2020.1438

40. Madjid M, Safavi-Naeini P, Solomon SD, Vardeny O. Potential effects of coronaviruses on the cardiovascular system: a review. JAMA Cardiol. 2020:5(7):831-840. DOI:10.1001/jamacardio.2020.1286

41. Mao L, Jin H, Wang M, et al. Neurologic manifistations of hospitalized patients with coronavirus disease 2019 in Wuhan, China. JAMA Neurol. 2020:77(6):683-690. DOI:10.1001/jamaneurol.2020.1127

42. Maragakis LL. Does wearing eye protection mitigate COVID-19 risk in public, non-healthcare settings? JAMA Ophthalmol. Published Online 11 September 2020. DOI:10.1001/jamaophthalmol.2020.3909

43. Mason DJ, Friese CR. Protecting healthcare workers against COVID-19—and being prepared for future pandemics. JAMA Health Forum. 2020:1(3):e200353. DOI:10.1001/jamahealthforum.2020.0353

44. Massachusetts Department of Public Health (MDPH) weekly influenza update 22 May 2020: estimated weekly severity of influenza. Online Accessed 8 July 2020. https://www.mass.gov/doc/weekly-flu-report-may-22-2020/download

45. Massachusetts Department of Public Health COVID-19 dashboard–30 April 2020. Accessed 8 July 2020. https://www.mass.gov/doc/COVID-19-dashboard-april-30-2020/download

46. MDedge. Clinical Endocrinology News, 1 September 2020:15(9).

47. Merkler AE, Parikh NS, Mr S, et al. Risk of ischemic stroke in patients with coronavirus disease 2019 (COVID-19) vs patients with influenza. JAMA Neurol. Published Online 2 July 2020. DOI:10.1001/jamaneurol.2020.2730

48. New England Journal of Medicine, editors. Death from COVID-19 of 23 healthcare Workers in China. N Engl J Med. 2020:382:2267-2268. DOI:10.1056/ NEJMc2005696

49. Nundy S, Patel KK. Self-service diagnosis of COVID-19—ready for prime time? JAMA Health Forum. 2020:1(3):e200333. DOI:10.1001/jamahealthforum. 2020.0333

50. Parke DW II. Ophthalmology after coronavirus disease 2019 (COVID-19): transition back to patient care. JAMA Ophthalmol. 2020:138(6):599-600. DOI:10.1001/ jamaophthalmol.2020.2004

51. Parker JD, Talih M, Malec DJ, et al. National Center for Health Statistics data presentation standards for proportions. Vital Health Stat 2. 2017:2(175):1-22.

52. Patel A, Jernigan DB; 2019-nCoV CDC Response Team. Initial public health response and interim clinical guidance for the 2019 novel coronavirus outbreak— United States, December 31, 2019-February 4, 2020. 2020:69(5):140-146. DOI:10.15585/mmwr. mm6905e1

53. Politi LS, Salsano E, Grimaldi M. Magnetic resonance imaging alteration of the brain in a patient with coronavirus disease 2019 (COVID-19) and anosmia. JAMA Neurol. 2020:77(8):1028-1029 DOI:10.1001/jamaneurol.2020.2125

54. Puntmann VO, Carerj ML, Wieters I, et al. Outcomes of cardiovascular magnetic resonance imaging in patients recently recovered from COVID-19 illness. JAMA Cordial. Published Online 27 July 2020. DOI:10.1001/jamacardio.2020.3557

55. Rezoagli E, McNicholas B, Pham T, et al. Lung-kidney cross-talk in the critically ill. Intensive Care Med. 2020:46(5):1072-1073. DOI:10.1007/s00134-020-05962-2

56. Roca-Gines J, Torres-Navarro I, Sanchez-Arraez J, et al. Assessment of acute acral lesions in a case series of children and adolescents during the COVID-19 pandemic. JAMA Dermatol. Published Online 25 June 2020 DOI:10.1001/jamadermatol.2020.2340

57. Santoriello D, Khairallah P, Bomback AS, et al. Postmortem kidney pathology findings in patients with COVID-19. J Am Soc Nephrol. 2020:31(9):2158-2167. DOI:10.1681/ASN.2020050744

58. Shi S, Qin M, Shen B, et al. Association of cardiac injury with mortality in hospitalized patients with COVID-19 in Wuhan, China. JAMA Cardiol. 2020:5(7):802-810. DOI:10.1001/jamacardio.2020.0950

59. Solomon IH, Normandin E, Bhattacharyya S, el al. Neuropathological features of COVID-19. N Engl J Med. Publishd Online 12 June 2020. DOI:10.1056/NEJMc2019373

60. Sommer A. Humans, viruses, and the eye—an early report from the COVID-19 front line. JAMA Ophthalmol. 2020:138(5):578-579. DOI:10.1001/jamaophthalmol.2020.1294

61. Sommer A. Humans, viruses, and the eye-an early report from the COVID-19 front line. JAMA Ophthalmol. 2020:138(5):578-579. DOI:10.1001/jamaophthalmol.2020.1294

62. Stephenson J. Coronavirus outbreak—an evolving public health emergency. JAMA Health Forum. 2020:1(2):e200114. DOI:10.1001/jamahealthforum.2020.0114

63. Su H, Yang M, Wan C, et al. Renal histopathological analysis of 26 postmortem findings of patients with COVID-19 in China. Kidney Int. 2020:98(1):219-227. DOI:10.1016/j.kint.2020.04.003

64. Wang X, Ferro EG, Zhou G, Hashimoto D, Bhatt DL. Association between universal masking in a healthcare system and SARS-CoV-2 positivity among healthcare workers. JAMA. Published Online 14 July 2020. DOI:10.1001/jama.2020.12897

65. Whittaker E, Bamford A, Kenny J, et al; PIMS-T5 Study Group and EUCLIDS and PERFORM Consortia. Clinical characteristics of 58 children with a pediatric inflammatory multisystem syndrome temporally associated with SARS-CoV-2. JAMA. 2020:324(3):259-269. DOI:10.1001/jama.2020.10369

66. Woolf SH, Chapman DA, Sabo RT, Weinberger DM, Hill L. Excess deaths from COVID-19 and other causes, March-April 2020. JAMA. Published Online 1 July 2020, DOI:10.1001/jama.2020.11787

67. World Health Organization (WHO). Mental health & COVID-19. Accessed 3 November 2020. https://www.who.int/teams/mental-health-and-substance-use/covid-19

68. World Health Organization (WHO). Website and other communication. 2020. https://www.who.int/

69. Wu P, Duan F, Luo C, et al. Characteristics of ocular findings of patients with coronavirus disease 2019 (COVID-19) in Hubei Province, China. JAMA Ophthalmol. 2020:138(5):575-578. DOI:10.1001/jamaophthalmo1.2020.1291

70. Zeng W, Wang X, Li J, et al. Association of daily wear of eyeglasses and susceptibility to COVID-19 infection. JAMA Ophthalmol. Published Online 11 September 2020. DOI:10.1001/jamaophthalmol.2020.3906

71. Zhang H, Dimitrov D, Simpson L, et al. A web-based, mobile responsive application to screen healthcare workers for COVID symptoms: descriptive study. Print 22 April 2020. DOI:10.1101/2020.04.17.20069211

72. Zubair AS, McAlpine LS, Gardim T, Farhadian S, Kuruvilla DE, Spuducg S. Neuropathogenesis and neurologic manifestations of the coronaviruses in the age of coronavirus disease 2019: a review. JAMA Neurol. 2020:77(8):1018-1027. DOI:10.1001/jamaneurol.2020.2065

Maha Abboud, MD, FACE

Born in Syria, award winning physician and clinical assistant professor Maha Abboud attended medical school at Damascus University. When she came to America for further education and training at Christ Hospital, University of Illinois, and Northwestern University, she fell in love with the country, and paved the way for her large family to enjoy what America has to offer. Maha has a flourishing medical practice. She served as an essential worker during the 2020 pandemic.

Maha founded both a unique weight loss program (Weigh Less for Way Less) and an education company (Live & Learn). In 2017, she co-authored *The Elephant in the Room: The Ultimate Guide to Weight Loss and Healthy Living*.

Maha has one daughter and two stepdaughters, has traveled the world (will continue to travel when able), and lives in the suburban Chicago area with her husband.